Privatization and the penal system

Privatization and the penal system

THE AMERICAN EXPERIENCE AND THE DEBATE IN BRITAIN

Mick Ryan and Tony Ward

Open University Press

MILTON KEYNES

Open University Press
12 Cofferidge Close
Stony Stratford
Milton Keynes MK11 1BY

First Published 1989

British Library Cataloguing in Publication Data

Ryan, Mick, *1941*–
    Privatization and the penal system: the
    American experience and the debate in Britain.
    – (Crime, justice and social policy)
    1. Great Britain. Prisons
    I. Title   II. Ward, Tony *1957*–
    III. Series
    365′.941

    ISBN 0-335-09916-5
    ISBN 0-335-09915-7 (pbk)

Typeset by Rowland Phototypesetting Ltd
Bury St Edmunds, Suffolk
Printed in Great Britain by St Edmundsbury Press Ltd
Bury St Edmunds, Suffolk

Contents

Foreword

The privatization of state-run institutions has become a dominant political issue in the 1980s. In the UK, the Conservative Government has privatized a number of state-controlled industries including British Gas, Telecom, Steel and Airways. It has actively supported this denationalization with the privatization and contracting out of public services such as refuse collecting, hospital cleaning and transport provision. In addition, Ministers have introduced legislation which allows private companies and individuals to be involved in determining policies around public housing, state schools and institutions of higher education, while simultaneously individual citizens are encouraged to obtain private health insurance for themselves, education for their children and nursing care for their parents. From the cradle to the grave, individuals are being pushed towards the private sector rather than relying on the 'Nanny' state built on the ideology of post-war social reconstruction which, it has been argued, encouraged a culture of dependency and apathy.

This first wave of privatization has been followed by similar proposals for the future denationalization of other institutions in state and civil society. Water, electricity, coal and the railway network are likely to be privatized before the next general election. It is in this second wave that the privatization of the prison system is being suggested.

This book is concerned with critically evaluating the issues in the debate around privatizing prisons, to move behind the rhetoric and explore the reality of privatization. Mick Ryan and Tony Ward provide, for the first time, a critical and in-depth analysis of this debate. They trace the emergence of private prisons in the USA, assess the experience of privately run prisons in that country and indicate how the reality of privatization falls far short of the rhetoric of financial savings, high standards, rehabilitation and reduced prison numbers.

Despite such fundamental problems, the British Government, through the publication of a Home Office Green Paper in July 1988, has confirmed its support for privatizing prisons. Ryan and Ward demonstrate the various influences on the Home Secretary's thinking. In particular, they assess the impact of the Third and Fourth Reports by the House of Commons Home Affairs Committee which after one corporately cocooned visit to the USA recommended that privatization should proceed in the UK.

As the book illustrates, this recommendation masks a host of ethical and political objections. These include the nature of the relationship between the state, the citizen and the limits to punishment; the issue of profit making and punishment; the connection between the interests of private capital and longer prison sentences, and the accountability of the private system in areas such as prison discipline. Ryan and Ward indicate that, given these issues, privatization is unlikely to solve the crisis in the penal system in Britain. They argue that there is a need for new, radical alternatives to prison, which carve out spaces in the machinery of penality and empower offenders to think critically and constructively about their behaviour. It is only through these processes directed from the 'bottom up' rather than incarceration in delapidated nineteenth-century institutions or surveillance by new-generation, high-tech buildings and electronic tags, that human behaviour can be changed positively.

This book provides not only the first overview of a central issue in penal politics but also indicates the direction for future monitoring and research in the area. Two issues are fundamental to such monitoring. First, the relationship between private prisons and the continuing expansion and accelerating centralization of state power. Private prisons, as Ryan and Ward's analysis suggests, will do little to challenge that expansion or the increasing authoritarianism demanded by capital-intensive, cost-effective regimes. Second, is the differential impact of privatization on separate areas of the penal estate. This includes the potential privatization of remand centres and the introduction of private services into women's prisons. Because women's prisons are seen to be at the 'soft' end of the system in terms of security the potential for private intervention and speculation in this area is even more pronounced. Additionally, because they are also few in number, women's prisons could be a favoured testing ground for privatization policies, thus legitimating further expansion and normalization in other areas of the penal system. The important issues which uniquely affect women such as welfare and medical services and mother and baby units are clearly of major importance in the debate around privatization and will need close monitoring.

The power of the state, and the limitations and accountability of that power, are key questions which will confront democracies in the 1990s and beyond. Private prisons are unlikely to challenge this material power. Neither will they subvert the powerful ideological construction which positions the state at the centre of penality, a matrix of closely linked individuals and institutions that have primacy in dispensing punishment. As Ryan and Ward indicate, this network of power can be challenged and dismantled only by the introduction of radical alternatives to prison geared to developing creative communities in which damaged and demoralized individuals can reconstruct their lives. Ryan and Ward's analysis, built on this strategy, fundamentally questions the discourses of retribution and discipline which underpin contemporary penal policy. At the same time, they provide the basis for the construction of a form of penality far different from that which lies at the heart of the privatization project.

Phil Scraton
Joe Sim
Paula Skidmore

Preface

In recent times there has been much argument in Britain and the USA over the question of privatizing prisons. This focus on the prison is to be expected. After all, the prison is still the show-piece of the modern penal apparatus, an apparently ever present, physical reminder of the state's awesome power to punish. While it is our clear intention to engage directly in this ongoing debate – indeed much of our book is about privatizing prisons as such – it is necessary at the outset to make the obvious point that there is far more to the modern penal apparatus than just prisons. There are, for example, halfway houses, probation hostels and re-entry centres for adults, to say nothing of the burgeoning number of community projects for juveniles which, in the USA in particular, almost defy enumeration.

While some radicals have recently criticized this apparent extension of punishment from the traditional closed space, the prison, into the community, it was generally welcomed during the late 1960s and early 1970s in progressive circles where it operated as a genuine alternative to imprisonment in large, degrading and costly institutions. The knowledge that many of the community-based projects which mushroomed at this time – halfway houses or whatever – were run by private organizations (or individuals) was also generally welcomed, or at least easily tolerated by progressives. The argument was that these alternatives offered a partly protected space for offenders who would otherwise be directly controlled by the agents of the state. Indeed, it would be fair to say that keeping the great Leviathan at bay and returning punishment to the community became one of the main objectives of most progressive groups in the penal lobby on both sides of the Atlantic.

This radical strategy was partly the echo of a far wider political movement. During this period what came to be known collectively (and loosely) as the New Left largely boycotted the institutions of the bourgeois state. A variety of parties and loosely organized groups voiced demands over a wide range of issues, including prisoners' rights, while standing outside, or apart from, the formal apparatus of the state which was taken to be inherently oppressive and irrelevant to the process of securing fundamental social and political change.

We recall this strategy because the recent suggestion that the responsibility for delivering punishment, especially in prisons, should in many cases be transferred from the state to private interests has caused deep misgivings in the penal lobby. Progressive groups like the National Prison Project of the American Civil Liberties Union have campaigned against it at state and federal levels. In Britain, where the state has managed and controlled all prisons from the centre since 1877, virtually the entire penal lobby has opposed privatization, from the prisoners' union PROP to the more traditional Howard League. It should be stressed that this progressive opposition was not only, nor primarily, based on the fact that all these groups had little faith in prisons as such, private or public, believing that most of them could easily be closed without any real danger or loss to the community. The main thrust of criticism was directed rather at privatization *per se*, at the very idea that the state might take such a determined step back from directing and controlling the penal apparatus. Suddenly, or so it seemed, the great Leviathan was back in favour, the applauded antithesis to privatization.

It was in response to this apparent paradox that this book was first conceived. The paradox is partly explained by the fact that the heady radical optimism of the late 1960s and early 1970s has long since evaporated and that the state is no longer totally written off by the Left as a vehicle for securing major social change or seen as something that has to be countered at every turn in order that an alternative society might grow and flourish. But to accept such a general explanation and leave the argument there would be to ignore more specific and difficult questions facing those who wish to engage in some form of radical intervention. What we intend to do in this book, therefore, is to look again at the penal apparatus and see if we can think through from a progressive perspective what the proper role of the state should be, where its authority should begin and end, and also to consider far more precisely what is meant by privatization and what might be acceptable in terms of private involvement and what might not. These are important questions of strategy which have to be addressed and which necessarily require that we look again, among other things, at the relationship between the state and the voluntary sector.

It should soon become clear that the call to privatize the delivery of punishment has not thrown up problems of definition and practice only for those who like to define their penal politics as radical or progressive, far from it. While to some supporters of the New Right in Britain the idea of privatizing certain categories of prison, say those holding illegal immigrants, is seen as acceptable, other more traditional Conservatives are far less convinced that even in these instances what they take to be the necessary levels of accountability and security can be guaranteed. So even among those on the Right who are ideologically committed from a Conservative standpoint to checking the advance of the great Leviathan, there are doubts about privatizing prisons, doubts which sometimes buttress radical or progressive anxieties.

It is, then, a complex and at times overlapping debate and one which involves ethical, legal and political considerations which belong to the public domain; their discussion cannot simply be left to those who would make money out of privatizing the delivery of punishment, whether they be private construction companies like McAlpine and Mowlem in Britain or brokers like Merill Lynch in the USA. Nor can we take it for granted that what might be acceptable penal practice in America is necessarily appropriate to Britain. It is for these reasons that we have written this book.

It will soon become obvious to anyone who looks critically at our work that our evaluation of the American experience of privatizing punishment is lacking in one crucial dimension, the offender's voice. What offenders, especially those on the inside, feel about being guarded by those on a private payroll obviously matters: they know where the shoe pinches, what the experience is really like. We were unable to fill this gap for a number of reasons, such as the absence of an authentic prisoners' movement to relay their voice and the very many practical obstacles which prevented us from conducting our own systematic enquiries. True, there was plenty of secondhand or anecdotal evidence, such as 'They love the food' or 'They don't really understand the arguments.' But such evidence is hardly adequate and the fact that some commentators have been prepared to use it probably reflects how little store they put by what prisoners think. Indeed, we have been struck by how few commentators on the American scene, especially academics, have worried about this gap in their evaluation of privatizing punishment, a gap which we feel must surely diminish our own work.

This gap aside, we have collected much information and received much help, and we would like to thank the following sources, first in North America and then in Europe.

We are particularly grateful to the Department of Political Science at the University of Akron, Ohio, where Mick Ryan was based for just over four months in 1988. The facilities made available for our research were extensive and members of the Department gave generously of their time to explain the political, legal and financial contexts in which the American penal system operates. We are particularly grateful to Steve Brooks, Bette Hill, Jesse Marquette, Carl Lieberman and Chris Smith. Graduate student Jan Grell also helped where and when she could and Mari Bell and Bonnie competently and willingly typed our many letters.

While we were in North America we also shared ideas (and information) about privatizing punishment with a number of other people and although it would be impossible for us to mention them all, we would like to acknowledge the following: Sharon A. Williams and Douglas W. Thomas (National Institute of Justice, Washington, DC); Bob Bohm (Jacksonville State University); Francis T. Cullen (University of Cincinnati); Russ Immarigeon (Maine Council of Churches); Ed Katz (Prisoners' Rights Project, Legal Aid Society, New York); Charles Logan (University of Connecticut); Maeve McMahon (University of Toronto); Dennis Palumbo (Arizona State University); Chris Stone (Vera Institute) and Robert Weiss (State University of New York).

At an institutional level we would like to single out the National Criminal

Justice Reference Center whose staff at Rockville competently dealt with our many enquiries.

We gathered more information than we were eventually able to use from the Netherlands and France and for this we would like to thank Rene van Swaaningen (Erasmus University, Rotterdam) and Frederique and Maurice at Liberation (Paris).

Turning to Britain, we owe a particular debt to Mike Nellis (University of Sheffield) whose ideas on the voluntary sector's role in the penal system have had an important influence on our own. Melissa Benn, David Brown, David Downes and Denis Jones read all or part of the manuscript and gave us helpful advice. The following people assisted us in our inquiries in various ways: Ruth Allan, Bron Roberts and Sally Swift (Labour Campaign for Criminal Justice); Gerry Bermingham MP; Rob Beynon (ITN); David Clelland MP; Rachel Hodgkin (Children's Legal Centre); John Hunt MP; Cathy Lloyd; David Plant (MATSA); Emily Russell and Frances Crook (Howard League); Stephen Shaw and Una Padel (Prison Reform Trust); Allison Skinner (National Youth Bureau); Chris Smith MP; Ivor Stanbrook MP; Vivien Stern (NACRO); Tim Tate; Max Taylor (University College, Cork); John Wheeler MP and Tony Worthington MP. The advice of the series editors Joe Sim, Phil Scraton and Paula Skidmore, and of John Skelton at the Open University Press, was as literate as their names are alliterative. Dave Leadbetter at INQUEST patiently tolerated his colleague's obsession with this project. The librarians at Thames Polytechnic were most helpful, especially Imogen Forster. Joan Ryan, as ever, gave sustained intellectual support.

Finally, we should like to extend our thanks to the restaurant where much of this book was conceived: the Mille Pini, Boswell Street, London.

CHAPTER 1

Setting the scene

IDEOLOGY AND PRAGMATISM

The recent suggestion that the delivery of punishment should be privatized ought not to surprise us. During the last two decades or so ideas about the role of the state have undergone a significant change in several leading Western democracies. In the USA there has been pressure at both federal and state levels to reduce public expenditure by investigating new and more efficient ways of running public services based on private business practices and, wherever possible, hiving off public functions to the private sector. In this drive to 'roll back the state' the federal government itself has taken a leading role. President Reagan's Reform 88 initiative was especially designed to bring public management practices more into line with those employed in business, while his Task Force on Private Sector Initiatives was specifically intended to involve the private sector more directly in the delivery of hitherto public services.[1] This political initiative from the centre has been well received by the private sector and entrepreneurs continue to come forward with their own schemes to diminish 'big government' and augment their corporate profits.

Despite important differences in governmental structure, and while the impact of private sector practices on the management of state agencies is less clear, it is easy to see parallels between the British and the American experience. Through a series of Stock Exchange flotations of public utilities such as gas and telecommunications, Mrs Thatcher's Conservative governments have transferred a whole range of industries and services back to the private sector.[2] Stringent controls on expenditure at local government level have also been introduced and a number of Conservative controlled authorities have been supported in their efforts to privatize local services such as refuse disposal. Even the regional health authorities which run Britain's socialized medical services have been forced to accept private tendering for hospital cleaning.

What all this suggests is that on both sides of the Atlantic privatization has

1

come to occupy a very important place on the political agenda of the New Right. So much so, perhaps, that it would not be unreasonable to argue that privatizing the delivery of punishment is nothing out of the ordinary, but just one more step along a clearly discernible path. While we would not go this far ourselves, since for a number of reasons we take the delivery of punishment to be anything but an ordinary function, we do accept that the call for privatization takes its rationale from a much wider ideological commitment. To put the argument more directly, it is on the agenda because the New Right want the state to do less as a matter of principle.

In the case of law and order, however, there is something of a paradox in the New Right's position, since they also want the state to do more to control those whose activities pose a threat to the orderly functioning of the free market, be they 'terrorists', 'rioters', trade union 'extremists' or just 'common criminals'. For the New Right, as Andrew Gamble points out, 'A minimal state does not mean a weak state. On the contrary, the state has to be strong to secure the conditions in which a free economy can work.'[3] The thought that the free market might itself be able to provide some of the hardware of the strong state is a further ideological attraction of prison privatization.

In tandem with this wider ideological commitment, however, is the claim that privatization offers a quick, cost-effective solution to many of the problems which face Western penal systems, particularly those in America and Britain. Whether this claim is justified or not is one of the many issues we intend to explore in later chapters. In the meantime, however, we do not quarrel with the assertion that Western penal systems have been experiencing problems – to put it mildly – or that something needs to be done soon if another Santa Fe (1980) or Peterhead (1986) is to be avoided.

In the USA the prison system was already under severe strain in the early 1980s. As a consequence, medical, sanitary and other essential services could not be guaranteed, while other less essential services such as educational classes were severely curtailed. A Bureau of Justice Statistics *Bulletin* reported that at local level 22 per cent (134) of America's largest jails (those with a capacity of over 100) were under court order in 1984 to expand capacity or reduce the number of inmates held and 24 per cent (150) were under court order to improve one or more of their conditions of confinement.[4] Three years later a research brief from the Bureau also reported that 60 per cent of all states were under court order to reduce prison overcrowding.[5] In an attempt to alleviate this chronic overcrowding and to comply with court orders the 1980s witnessed one of the biggest prison building programmes in American history; at one time more than a hundred new facilities were planned at an estimated cost of 3.5 billion dollars.[6] The impact of this planned investment has yet to materialize. Indeed, the US Department of Justice paints a desperate picture. Its Director writes:

The crisis in our streets has become the crisis in our prisons. Fear of crime and increased feelings of vulnerability have hardened public attitudes and led to higher penalties for criminals. The number of criminals in prison passed the half a million mark last year, an increase of 50 per cent in five years. Struggling to keep pace with the prison explosion [some] States are currently under court order to reduce the overcrowding or run the risk of releasing hardened criminals before the end of their prison term.[7]

While the Prison Department in Britain is protected by a number of mechanisms from similar legal challenges, its problems are not dissimilar. The prison population has now reached record levels and there is severe overcrowding, particularly in local remand centres where living conditions are appalling.[8] In an attempt to relieve this overcrowding the prison department is launched on its biggest prison building programme this century. A total of 26 new prisons is planned, of which 6 are already built and in use. The Department has also begun an extensive programme of refurbishment in an effort to bring the existing prison stock up to standard.[9]

This expansion of the prison system on both sides of the Atlantic is using valuable financial resources, resources which the British and American governments would prefer to leave in the taxpayer's pocket. It is mainly because of this that there is talk of private sector involvement in the delivery of punishment, which it is hoped will help to reduce what governments have to spend on their respective prison systems. Moreover, expanding the prison system is taking far longer than both governments would like or can afford, so an additional attraction of private sector involvement is the claim that its involvement will speed up the provision of additional prison places.

The rationale for involving the private sector in the delivery of punishment is therefore both ideological and pragmatic; it is urged on both governments as a solution to the existing penal crisis in a form which appeals to their basic political instincts about limiting the role of the state. It is important to stress at this point that no one, except perhaps a few 'anarcho-capitalists', is suggesting that the state through Parliament, Congress or the judiciary should give up its monopoly over the *allocation* of punishment – or more accurately certain kinds of punishment.[10] There are, of course, many kinds of private justice and employers, schools, parents and so forth can punish people by a variety of physical and economic means; but few would challenge the idea that only the state should be able to impose punishments which require the organized use of force on any substantial scale, such as imprisonment, the death penalty or punishments like probation which are backed by the threat of imprisonment for non-compliance.[11] All that is being argued is that the *delivery* of some of these punishments might be entrusted to private agencies in one form or another. The exact nature of these private agencies – their financial basis – is something we shall come to shortly. In the meantime, however, let us consider what private involvement might amount to in practice, starting with the prison system.

THE SCOPE OF PRIVATIZATION

Privatization can take many forms: it might mean that a private company builds, staffs and then runs a prison, receiving its clients, as it were, from the courts or indirectly from elsewhere in the penal system; or it could mean that a private company or some other entity builds a prison and then rents it to the government of the day which then operates it with its own staff in the usual way. As governments are deeply concerned about the running costs of existing prisons, privatization might also take the form of contracting out to private sector companies certain services, perhaps the provision of food or medicine. There are also prison industries. Could they be made more profitable if they were taken away from the prison authorities? Entrepreneurs might be invited to run or set up prison-based industries or even hire out prisoners as contract labour to work for nearby companies. These are just some of the ways in which private sector companies could become involved in the prison system.

While prison is the deep end of the penal system, we have already made the point that the modern penal system is a complex one with many different parts. At the shallower end there are institutions such as community or juvenile homes, halfway houses, bail hostels, community-based projects and a whole host of smaller sites for the delivery of punishment. And, of course, private interests have been involved in running many of these sites since the nineteenth century. In this context, then, we might well ask what is new about privatizing the delivery of punishment. There are basically two answers to this very important question. The first is that while the *modern* penal system is indeed varied and flexible, the deep end of the system, and prisons in particular, has traditionally been run by the state. The suggestion that private companies might now operate in this space is new and open to numerous objections, as we shall see. Second, most of the interests involved in running the shallow end of the system have traditionally been non-profit agencies, whereas those interests now bidding to run prisons are companies whose corporate interest is first and foremost to secure profit.

We should make it clear that we do not take a simple view of this divide, arguing for example that what is done by non-profit agencies is somehow necessarily good and desirable, while that which is done by profit seeking companies is automatically undesirable. Far from it, what was done by non-profit agencies to lock up children in the nineteenth century in both the USA and Britain was undesirable by any standards.[12] Also, it is well to remember that there are profit-making agencies operating at the shallow end of the system – some halfway houses and juvenile facilities, for example – while in some areas of America non-profit companies have been formed to run prison industries. The boundaries are not altogether tightly drawn. To make this point is not to suggest that there is no clearly discernible, non-profit or voluntary sector in Britain and the USA. There clearly is and we intend to touch on the very real differences between the American and British penal systems in this respect and make some assessment of their respective contributions. It may well be that the delivery of punishment in this sector offers more space for radical intervention than is available in the formal penal system. This suggests a possible strategy which we already know is full of pitfalls but is at least worth re-working in the context of the current debate.

4

THE BRITISH AND AMERICAN SYSTEMS

We should finally like to make some preliminary observations on the difference between the American and British penal systems. The first and most obvious characteristic of the British system is that it is highly centralized and that it has been so for over a century. In 1877 responsibility for all local and county prisons was transferred, overnight, to central government in the form of the Prison Commission. The prison service thus became, as the Webbs noted, the most unified and centralized social service in Britain.[13] No other service – education, medicine or even public health – was so comprehensively nationalized. Over the years the Prison Commission became absorbed into the Home Office which has an elected national politician – a senior member of the majority party – at its head who is answerable to Parliament for what goes on in the penal system.[14] The penal system is also centrally funded and the money which is voted by Parliament each year comes out of general tax revenues and/or from the government's borrowing on the market. There is no financial input at either local or county (state) levels. Indeed, there is no local control over local prisons at all. Local health departments cannot inspect them nor do local politicians have any say in how they are run. The rules and regulations about staffing, prison routines and the like are laid down from the centre and there is a centrally organized inspectorate to oversee prison administration. True, local lay persons – appointed from the centre – make up Boards of Visitors to adjudicate on questions of internal discipline and generally oversee the running of prisons; but their powers are strictly limited.[15]

While the rigidity of this hierarchical system is anything but democratic and the penal lobby, rightly in our view, agitates to make it more publicly accountable, it is at least reasonably easy to see how it works. There is ultimately one legal authority and one source of finance. Quite the opposite is true in the USA where there are at least three levels of authority. There are federal prisons, which are funded from taxation at the centre, state prisons and local jails which are funded from their own revenues – property taxes, sales taxes and so forth. So, whereas in Britain the decision to build a new prison or jail would have no direct financial consequences for any local authority or state equivalent, the situation would be altogether different in the USA: the capital required would have to be raised locally by the responsible state or local authority, as would the revenue for its later running costs.

This fragmentation of authority also impacts on organized labour. American prison guards are neither as powerful nor as well organized at national level as their British counterparts where the militant Prison Officers' Association speaks with one voice for all guards below governor rank and can, therefore, quickly reduce the national prison system to a state of crisis if it chooses. These, of course, are not the only differences between the two systems. The difference which perhaps strikes British observers most keenly is the arrangement whereby local jails are run by democratically elected local sheriffs. In Britain those directly charged with running prisons are government officials, with the single exception of the career politician who nominally oversees the whole operation from the centre; and the idea that the day to day running of the system might be given over to people who have to stand for political office seems very odd indeed.

Some of the differences between the two penal systems which we have just outlined – and we will come across many more – are directly related to our present study. In the first place, the different and largely autonomous layers of authority which are found in the USA encourage diversity. Practices within states, between states or between the federal and other systems vary a good deal and this inevitably makes generalizations about what is happening in American penal practice difficult. This is a problem not only for outsiders like ourselves, but also for Americans; the need to investigate and publicize what individual prison authorities are doing in the USA is one of the important functions of the federally funded National Institute of Justice and its various associate bodies. So we need to be cautious. While generalizations can and must be made, American practice, especially when it comes to major innovations like privatization, could well turn out to be sketchy and uneven.

How far American practice has so far been understood and used in the British debate on privatizing the delivery of punishment is also something we wish to investigate. There are strong links between the two countries. We share a common heritage and a common language. There is, it is often said, a special relationship and it is therefore no wonder that what is happening in America is of constant interest to us in Britain. In important ways, however, this relationship is not an equal one, as Stuart Hall *et al.* have pointed out.[16] America is taken to be the future: 'What is happening over there will soon be happening over here.' To take two not uninteresting examples in the context of our present study, the American labels mugging and yuppy – with all that they signified about urban lawlessness hand in hand with the so-called enterprise culture – have predictably turned up in Britain. This process of transference, however, is a complicated one. Ideas and practices cross the Atlantic in many different forms and their impact is necessarily mediated by British customs, institutions and beliefs. An investigation of this process will uncover several different interests at work; pressure groups, politicians and the media have all had an important role to play in interpreting the American experience. It is on this experience that we focus next.

NOTES

1. National Institute of Justice, *The Privatization of Corrections*, Washington, DC, 1985, Chapter 1.
2. The Treasury's annual privatization target is reported to be around five billion pounds.
3. A. Gamble, *Britain in Decline* (1981), cited in P. Scraton, 'Unreasonable force', in P. Scraton (ed.), *Law, Order and the Authoritarian State*, Open University Press, Milton Keynes, 1987.
4. National Institute of Justice, *Systemwide Strategies to Alleviate Jail Overcrowding*, Washington, DC, 1987.
5. National Institute of Justice, *Contracting for the Operation of Prisons and Jails*,

Washington, DC, 1987. In the USA local jails are normally used for people who have committed minor offences or who are awaiting trial and cannot afford bail. Prisons, on the other hand, are either the responsibility of state or federal authorities and are used for those who have committed serious offences or felonies.

6. M. Moerings, 'Prison overcrowding in the United States', in B. Rolston and M. Tomlinson (eds), *The Expansion of European Prison Systems*, EDC, Belfast, 1986.

7. *Op. cit.*, note 5.

8. In July 1987 the number of prisoners in England and Wales stood at 50,969, the highest prison population on record.

9. *Private Sector Involvement in the Remand System*, HMSO, London, 1988, para. 10.

10. For example, M. N. Rothbard, *For a New Liberty: The Libertarian Manifesto*, Collier/Macmillan, New York, 1978.

11. S. Henry, *Private Justice*, Routledge, London, 1983; C. D. Shearing and P. C. Stenning (eds), *Private Policing*, Sage, Newbury Park and London, 1987.

12. For the American experience, see A. M. Platt, *The Childsavers: The Invention of Delinquency*, University of Chicago Press, Chicago, 1969. For Britain see *Law and Disorder: Histories of Crime and Justice*, Part 4, *Youth and Reforming Zeal*, Open University Press, Milton Keynes, 1981.

13. S. J. Webb and B. Webb, *English Prisons Under Local Government*, Longman, London, 1922.

14. The Scottish prison system is organized separately and is the responsibility of the Secretary of State for Scotland, who is also a member of the Cabinet.

15. For some discussion of their role, see M. Maguire, J. Vagg and R. Morgan (eds), *Accountability and Prisons*, Tavistock, London, 1965.

16. S. Hall *et al.*, *Policing the Crisis*, Macmillan, London, 1976.

CHAPTER 2

The American experience

We referred in Chapter 1 to the pressure on Western penal systems and how this has led to the demand for more prison building. We also pointed out that there was a call for meeting this demand in a particular way, that is by privatizing the delivery of punishment, a solution which has a strong ideological appeal to the New Right. We did not ask why the demand for prison places had grown or discuss possible alternative ways of relieving the pressure. Yet these are clearly fundamental questions. We cannot assume that demand is unproblematic or that constructing new prisons, whether built and/or managed by either the public or the private sector, is inevitable. It is partly because of the need to signal these problems that we have chosen to begin this chapter by looking briefly at the prison crisis in New York State (though it is important to remember our earlier warning that there is nowhere that is typically 'American'). In addition, and central to our present concern, this will tell us something about how prison building is funded in the USA and how the present pressure on the penal system offers opportunities for corporate investors. This will be followed by a report on other aspects of the privatization debate in America, such as the use of prison labour by the private sector, the contracting out of prison services and the place of private interests at the shallow end of the penal system. We will then discuss opposition to privatization and attempt to assess how far the process has gone.

The problem faced by New York can be guessed at if we first consider the size and growth of its prison population. In 1974 there were 14,000 prisoners. By 1983/4 this figure had climbed steadily to reach 32,926. Spending through the State Purpose Operations Budget on prisons and prison services rose from approximately 192.7 million dollars in 1974 to approximately 523.5 million dollars in 1983/4.[1] This massive increase in expenditure did little to alleviate tensions on the inside. In 1976 there were prisoner strikes at Attica, Green Haven and Great Meadows. A year later 17 hostages were taken at Eastern Penitentiary. In 1983 there was still more trouble at Attica and during the

Ossining (Sing Sing) disturbances 19 hostages were held before a peaceful settlement was negotiated.

The response of New York prison administrators to this pressure was to demand even more resources. They argued that overcrowding was the main problem and that the provision of more prison space was therefore the only solution. This simple interpretation of New York's problem has been criticized by James Fox, who suggests that the prison crisis has been caused by tougher sentences, by racism throughout the criminal justice system, coercion and intimidation on the inside and the increasingly desperate plight of New York's underclass. All these factors he sees as stemming from, or being exacerbated by, the ascendancy of the New Right.[2] We are in no position to say for sure whether Fox is correct. We would, for example, welcome a more thorough investigation of New York's crime rates. It will, however, become clear as this book unfolds that we are very much in favour of an analysis of the present penal crisis which goes beyond simply counting heads and spaces and instead looks far more critically at the criminal justice system as a whole and the wider political and economic environment in which it operates. To do otherwise is to give in to the New Right's law and order rhetoric and, more to the present point, to throw good money after bad. We would like to think that it was one, or both, of these considerations that led the citizens of New York State to defeat the 1981 prison bond proposal. It is to this proposal and the funding of American prisons generally that we now turn.

FROM CREDIT CARDS
TO PRISONS

Given the increase in New York's prison population and the heads and spaces mentality of its prison administrators, it will come as no surprise to learn that more prison places were pressed for and won. Something like 5,000 additional places were provided between 1973 and 1979 alone by converting buildings previously used for other purposes. It was only when an additional 3–5,000 places were being planned for around 1980 that the method of financing this expansion came under legislative scrutiny and the state was forced to seek public approval through a referendum to raise money for new capital expenditure on prisons by issuing a prison bond.[3]

To British ears such a procedure seems very strange indeed. In the first place, as we have already noted, prison building is financed centrally. There is simply no way in which London or any local authority would be asked to finance new prison building or, indeed, renovate old ones. Second, duly elected governments in Britain – at every level – are allowed to exercise all their legally defined powers to raise taxation without first seeking the consent of their local electorates through referenda. True, they might occasionally raise more in taxation than their electorates were prepared to tolerate and subsequently be voted out of office; but that is quite another process. What they would never have to face was New York's predicament when the referendum to issue a prison bond was defeated.[4]

In very basic terms the American system works in the following way. While a few extra prison places – or school places for that matter – can usually be funded out of current revenues and while local and state governments are wise to fund new projects in this way where they can to avoid interest charges, large capital projects like new prisons have to be funded by raising money on the market by bond issues which usually (though not always) require voter approval. A survey by the National Institute of Justice carried out in 1984 showed that about 50 per cent of all states anticipated funding their prison construction programmes through bonds and another 10 per cent with a combination of bonds and current revenues.[5] In a word, long-term borrowing on the market was – and still is – the most popular way of financing prison construction.

It should be pointed out that there are two kinds of bond. Revenue bonds are repaid from various charges or fees, say where they are used to finance a toll bridge, and general obligation bonds are repaid out of state or local authority revenues. The former are less likely to be subject to voter approval than the latter, though it is these that are most commonly used to finance new prisons.[6] The continuing popularity of general obligation bonds is easy to understand: they spread the burden of capital expenditure over a number of years. But their issue is not always an option. In the first place, states and localities cannot simply borrow as they please. They are subject to debt limitation, not only to protect taxpayers from free spending politicians, but also to make sure that public officials do not secure too much debt against available resources; this would, among other things, damage the state or local authority's credit rating on the market. Second, as we saw in the case of New York, voters may not approve a particular bond issue. Other ways of raising money therefore have to be found and this has led to a number of lease financing alternatives. Enter American Express.

Briefly, what some states and local governments are considering, and what some have already done, is to lease prisons whose building has been financed through deals put together by brokerage houses and investment firms, blue chip firms like E. F. Hutton, Merrill Lynch and Shearson Lehman/American Express.[7] There are a number of ways in which these packages can be put together, important tax concessions secured and legal and constitutional obstacles to raising new money overcome.[8] For example, with the active participation of its Wall Street advisors, the local authority might set up a new entity which operates, in strictly legal terms, outside any debt limitation. This entity could raise the necessary finance, design and construct a prison and then lease it to the state or local government in question. After a period of years the ownership of the prison might pass to the state or the local government or stay with the lessor (possibly to be used for other purposes), depending on the exact nature of the lease negotiated. One of the earliest and best known lease purchase agreements was negotiated by Jefferson County, Colorado. In 1983, after local voters had twice rejected sales tax proposals to raise new funds, E. F. Hutton arranged a 30.2 million dollar lease purchase agreement for the county. The new prison for around 400 inmates was opened in 1985 and will be leased until 1995 when the debt is repaid.[9]

Straight lease arrangements obviously carry some risks for the private investor. If the prison population dropped the state or local government would have no need to renew its lease, leaving the lessor with a building which would probably be difficult and costly to convert and, because it was located in some remote spot away from the main centres of urban population, difficult to lease for other purposes. This is not a risk that too many investors are likely to take, even at a time when America's prison population is on the increase. Simply put, there are safer ways of making money.

It is important to remind ourselves at this point that not all state and local governments are looking to secure lease or lease purchases. In fact, it looks as if most of the money for new prisons is going to be raised in the traditional way. Where it remains an option this can turn out to be the cheapest deal on offer. For example, Minnesota rejected all private bids for the lease purchases of a women's prison because its good credit rating made general obligation bond financing more cost-effective. Officials estimated that the net cost of issuing general obligation bonds for the new prison would be something like nine million dollars less than taking up one of the proposals it had received for lease purchase financing![10] This sort of discrepancy prompted the National Institute of Justice to warn that there was no simple answer to the question, 'Are lease and lease purchase agreements the cheapest way of financing prison expansion?' A lot will depend on local circumstances. Nevertheless, what the National Institute of Justice did confirm was that such agreements were options to circumvent limitations placed on public expenditure. Even here, however, it sounded a cautionary note when explaining the legal problems New York ran into when it sought to evade the expressed wishes of the people:

> The avoidance of public referenda and debate through the issuance of revenue bonds and certificates has been said to conceal or obscure what governments are doing. Critics charge that the practice violates the spirit if not the letter of the law and the intended participation of the citizenry in decisions related to the policy choices and longterm obligations of their government. In New York a taxpayers' suit was filed against the Urban Development Corporation to prevent it from issuing bonds after a general obligation bond issue for correctional facilities failed at the polls. Ominously for lease purchase advocates the taxpayers won on the trial court level, but the state's highest court, the Court of Appeals, dismissed the complaint for lack of jurisdiction and allowed the Urban Development Corporation to proceed with the six hundred million dollar bond issue. It is impossible to estimate the generalizability of the New York precedent to other states now considering leasing alternatives.[11]

In other words, the judgement could just as easily go the other way.

What we have overall, then, is a still developing situation in which investment institutions are moving in, but by no means everywhere, to underwrite new, mainly local facilities. This development may seem logical in the American context, but given that there are no comparable democratic obstacles to financing new prisons in Britain, and that our system of tax exemptions is very different, it is difficult to see the same thing happening in Britain. Some variant might just conceivably be tried, with central government arguing that as its own resources are made up of taxation and what it borrows on the market, the private sector is already involved in the prison building programme through its purchase of government stocks. This is hardly a sufficient argument for privatizing the delivery of punishment; but it would at least allow the government in Britain to argue that looking to the private sector is not an intrinsically new departure.

It is finally worth pointing out that since they could expect to have a decisive imput into the design of new prisons and the supervision of their construction, this option is about as close as states and local government can get to the power they exercise when raising their own capital through general obligation bonds. However, whether this preferred cption will continue to be available is uncertain because the 1986 tax reform has tightened the restrictions on the non-governmental financing of government projects through tax exempt bonds.[12] Thus what we have already identified as a modest trend towards financing new prisons through lease or lease purchase arrangements may be even more modest in the future. It would be ironic if President Reagan's much heralded tax initiative turned out to limit the participation of the private sector in the delivery of public services, though we are as yet unable to be certain that this will happen.

Lease and lease purchase agreements may have their critics; but if they are put together in a way which leaves the state or local government very much in control they are far less controversial than those deals which allow private contractors to both build (or convert) prisons and then staff and run them, albeit within some publicly defined regulatory framework. Such deals have been struck with private entrepreneurs who are prepared to risk or venture their capital in this way in the hope of securing a good financial return. It is these deals we now consider, starting at the shallow end of the system with the detention of illegal immigrants.

FUNDING IMMIGRANT DETENTION

As a successful and wealthy country America has long attracted immigrants, both those who have registered and come legally and those who have sought to evade all immigration controls and slip in illegally. In recent times, however, and mainly as a result of the grinding poverty and political instability in Central America which it has helped to sustain, the American government has found it difficult to cope with the flow of illegal immigrants across its southern borders and as a result the Federal Immigration and Naturalization Service (INS) has turned to the private sector to provide at least five detention centres.[13]

Corrections Corporation of America (CCA) controls two of these centres. The largest is a purpose-built structure with only modest perimeter security at

Houston – where many Central and Latin American governments have consulates – which acts as a major deportation point. Built and designed by CCA and financed by venture capital, the centre holds 350 detainees. The Laredo centre, which is smaller with only 200 places, was also designed and built by CCA. The Corporation is wholly in charge of both operations – hiring and firing its own staff – and is in receipt of an annually renewable contract with the INS on the basis of *per diem* payments.[14] Another company, Behavioral Systems Southwest Incorporated, houses a further 350 detainees in converted motels in California, Arizona and Colorado.[15]

The Corrections Corporation of America achieved a certain notoriety because of its political and financial ancestry. Established in 1983 by a former chairman of the Tennessee Republican Party, Tom Beasley, it was originally financed by the Massey Birch Investment Group which came to public notice with its buy out of Kentucky Fried Chicken from the legendary Colonel Harlan Sanders. Critics of privatizing the delivery of punishment thus had a field day with headlines such as 'From Junk Food to Jails'. While such snappy headlines obviously serve a purpose, they should not obscure the fact that it was the Massey Birch Investment Group which started the now giant Hospital Corporation of America and that if he gets the chance Beasley intends to run CCA along similar lines, with bulk purchase orders, centralized management and accounting and the recruitment of personnel from public agencies for the day to day running of its facilities.[16] By the mid-1980s Beasley clearly felt that he was on the verge of something dynamic and noble and was quoted as saying, 'There are rare times when you get involved in something that is productive and profitable and humanistic. We're on the cutting edge of a brand new industry.'[17] The President and founder of Behavioral Systems Southwest Incorporated, Ted Nissen, seems less pretentious and much more matter of fact about his business, simply saying, to paraphrase the ubiquitous Colonel Sanders, that he has found something he can make a profit from and he intends to stick to it. A former employee of the California Corrections Department, Nissen reportedly once ran a non-profit making halfway house for heroin addicts before cashing in on punishment.[18]

It is not difficult to understand why the federal government has been prepared to loosen its grip on the delivery of punishment at this end of the system. In the first place, most illegal immigrants are normally jailed for only relatively short periods before they are deported. What is involved is basically a warehousing operation with little or no counselling or effort to rehabilitate. And, of course, the fact that most, though not all, immigrants have not transgressed the criminal law as such makes it easier for the state to step back without being accused of giving up one of its most important functions. The fact that immigrants have traditionally been seen as a low security risk also helps, though the riot of Cuban detainees at a federally run centre in Louisiana in 1987 may help to change this perception.[19] Nor should we forget that most detainees inevitably face routine daily abuses or frustrations, that is the nature of confinement. Moreover, the private sector containment of aliens has not been without serious abuses. For example, in 1981, 16 Colombians were handed over to Danner Incorporated, a private security company, which placed them in a 12 by 20 foot cell designed to hold six prisoners. After two days they tried to escape and in the process a private security guard shot and killed one detainee and wounded another.[20] A subsequent court action based on this tragic incident found that the contracting out of corrections still constituted state action, thus challenging the sometimes unstated premise of the privatization lobby that the private operation of prisons might limit government liability and so reduce its costs.[21] (When stated explicitly, the premise is usually translated into a promise by private operators to indemnify the state against any future legal action.[22])

Finally, it is worth emphasizing that the numbers involved are relatively small, in spite of the high media profile that some security companies operating in this field have cultivated. At present the total number of aliens being held by the private sector appears to be well under a thousand, which is still only a modest proportion of the total.[23] But for the reasons we have just outlined the temptation to expand at this end of the system remains and it is one which the British government has found difficult to resist, as we shall see.

CORRECTIONAL INSTITUTIONS

At the deep end of the American system the private sector is involved even less in building (or converting) and then running correctional institutions for profit, though there is some movement here which may turn out to be significant. In Kentucky the state legislature has made possible – as it is perfectly entitled to do without any reference to federal authority – what is being described as America's first private, adult state prison to be run as a profit making enterprise.[24] Kentucky was one of those states under court order to do something about its overcrowding. The company which both owns and runs Saint Mary is the United States Corrections Corporation and was originally financed by property developer J. Clifford Todd and architect Milton Thompson who negotiated a three-year state contract starting in January 1986.[25]

Saint Mary is set in rural Kentucky on a site previously developed as a college campus. There are no restraining fences and no weapons. The prisoners are all near parole eligibility and to an extent have been handpicked to allow the enterprise to begin trouble free. Thus, while the inmates have indeed been convicted of crimes, and Saint Mary is indeed a 'regular' prison, it is far from being at the really deep end of the system. Nevertheless, it does break new ground and other states might be tempted to legislate along similar lines. Here again the difference between the American and British systems is striking. Such an experiment could be authorized only by central government in Britain and any attempt to repeat or extend it would also be taken at the centre. Local or state penal initiatives at the deep end of the system are thus severely restricted in Britain: the legal framework effectively precludes them.

As it happens, there is not much evidence to suggest that other states are queuing up to emulate Kentucky, which is something of a disappointment for the private sector. CCA, for example, put in a bid to run the entire Tennessee prison system. This followed a federal court order to upgrade the state's prison facilities after a series of demonstrations in 1985 which led to the death of one inmate and damage to prison property of around 7.5 million dollars.[26] The company wanted a 99-year lease on the prison system which it would then run for an annually negotiated fee. This proposal was rejected by the state and CCA is now trying to secure contracts to run just one or two medium security prisons.[27]

Another ambitious proposal was put forward by Buckingham Security to build a prison in Beaver County, Pennsylvania. The estimated cost was between 15 and 20 million dollars and the proposal was to take prisoners on protective custody from elsewhere in the system. This caused a major controversy in Pennsylvania and the state legislature published a special *Report on a Study of Issues Related to the Operation of Private Prisons in Pennsylvania*. The outcome of the controversy was a defeat for Buckingham Security. There were many factors involved, including the background of one senior company member. It was revealed that Charles Fenton had served for some years in the federal prison system. He was warden of a prison in Lewisburg and in that capacity was found by a federal jury to have been among a group of prison officials who inflicted 'cruel and unusual punishment' on two inmates.[28]

Where private corporations have not been able to secure contracts to both build and run prisons they have been happy to settle for deals which simply involve them in management. For example, Florida's Bay County Correctional Centre, a mixed prison housing both pre-trial and convicted men and women, had a long history of health and safety violations and the county authorities seemed more than willing to reach an agreement with CCA to run the centre on the basis of *per diem* payments. In the face of overcrowding the county later contracted with CCA to construct a 4.5 million dollar 'work camp' which sounds quite awesome, with motion detectors, closed circuit cameras and sound sensors.[29] Another privately managed institution, and arguably the most well established, is the Weaversville intensive treatment unit in Pennsylvania run by the RCA Service Company. As at Bay County, the buildings remain public property, but those running the programme are RCA staff. The state sets minimum standards, however, and publishes a yearly budget, 5 per cent of which is RCA's profit. So far RCA has managed to operate within its budget and Weaversville has generally had a sympathetic press.[30] The same cannot be said of the Okeechobee School for hard core delinquents.

The Okeechobee experiment is worth looking at in some detail for several reasons. In the first place, privately run institutions in the juvenile sector are mostly modest operations. Weaversville, for example, caters for only about twenty hard core delinquents. Okeechobee, on the other hand, holds between 400 and 450 juveniles, many of whom have committed 'prison quality' offences. It is a large institution and was a real management test for the Eckerd Foundation which negotiated to run it for the state of Florida in 1982 at an annual charge of about six million dollars. The sheer scale of the operation attracted the attention of several interests outside Florida itself and the National Institute of Corrections (NIC) agreed to undertake an independent study of the experiment.[31] Although running Okeechobee was left to the non-profit making arm of the major US drug manufacturer, the Eckerd Corporation, the belief that the private sector could deliver a better and more cost-effective service was at the heart of the experiment and why, in cost conscious times, the NIC had a real interest in monitoring its operation.

There is little dispute that the Okeechobee experiment got off to a bad start. Even before the transfer to private management took place there were disturbing rumours about what might happen and the Florida Highway Patrol was requested to stand by in case of trouble.[32] When the Eckerd Foundation did eventually take over it seems clear that several wrong decisions were taken in the very early days. A significant number of custody and care staff – those who had agreed to stay on with the new management – were sacked and some others were asked to work 16 hours a day for reduced pay. The use of the polygraph or lie detector was also introduced and this added to the growing distrust between line staff and managers.[33] Staff morale slumped and on just about every important indicator the NIC used Okeechobee scored less well than the institution to which it was compared. So how did the NIC assess this important experiment overall? Its final report first raised, and then answered the following two questions:

1. Would Florida's Department of Health and Rehabilitative Services (which manages the juvenile training school system) realize substantial savings under the new management structure?
2. Would the Eckerd Foundation deliver a program which was equal to or exceeded that provided by the state?

In response to the first question; on balance, the fiscal data seem to indicate that the Eckerd Foundation achieved no significant reductions in operational costs . . . [and] concerning the second question . . . no fundamental differences were found in program comparisons between Okeechobee and Dozier (comparison institution) clients; and staff morale was significantly lower at Okeechobee. Improvements in a number of service delivery areas (at Okeechobee) were noted.[34]

In a word, while some advantages were secured from buying in certain goods and services, that was about the sum total on the plus side. These were early days, but there were no signals that the future would bring dramatic improvements or big financial savings.

The issue of savings is an important one and we shall return to it later in this chapter. In the meantime, however, it is important to make some overall assessment of what is happening in this area and to ask how far profit making providers and/or managers of penal institutions have penetrated the American market. The answer is not very far, at least at the deep end of the system. The research brief from the National Institute of Justice to which we referred in Chapter 1, and in which the Institute's Director reported that there were now over half a million persons in state and federal prison in the USA, also reported that 'approximately 1,200 adults are being held in secure correctional facilities privately operated for state and local governments in the United States'.[35] This total appears to include prisoners in institutions which were both financed, built and then operated by private companies (e.g. Saint Mary, Kentucky) and prisoners in institutions which are simply managed by private companies (e.g. the CCA operation at Silverdale, Tennessee). Even the very latest unofficial estimate from a pro-privatization source – and this appears to include juveniles in secure custody – puts the figure as low as 3,000.[36] This is slow progress by any standards, and given the size of the United States prison population hardly a significant contribution to relieving pressure on the system.

Perhaps the only real advance by the private sector on the building front – and this is to define the issue very narrowly – has been in the supply of prefabricated cells. The advantages of prefabricated cells seem to be obvious. It is claimed that they can be ordered, transported and erected in a relatively short time; and because they are prefabricated and factory-made they may cost less than conventionally built cells. They are also flexible in that it is suggested that they can be leased and then returned when the prison population drops. But there are drawbacks. For example, only a limited number of cells can reasonably be added to any prison or jail before they overload the main service systems such as drainage, medical and recreational space and so forth. Security is usually based on clear sight lines and these can be impaired if too many cells are added to the basic system. And, of course, there is little hard evidence as yet about the durability of these cells, or indeed about what the quality of life might be like in such uniform structures. The apparent willingness of some prison administrators to overlook these difficulties has led Sechrest et al. to warn about the dangers of being too easily taken in by 'entrepreneurial promotions' which make claims for prefabricated cells which have so far yet to be tested.[37] However, in spite of this recent and timely warning a number of companies like Gelco Space already have a toe in what looks like an expanding market.[38] Less inviting is the opportunity to use prison labour.

PRISON LABOUR

The idea that prison labour should be exploited for private profit is hardly new. In America during the nineteenth century such exploitation was widespread, even if the manner in which it was practised varied from state to state. In an attempt to contextualize the present debate and also to explain how and why the exploitation of prison labour by private interests came to be severely restricted we intend to sketch briefly some of the practices which were once in use.

It is generally agreed that the worst and most profitable form of exploitation involved was the lease system. Under this arrangement the state or some other public authority entered into a contract with a private lessee – it could be an individual or a company – who agreed to house, feed and clothe the prisoners, prevent them from escaping and in return use their labour to cover his or the company's initial outlay and secure a profit. In return the state received an agreed sum.[39] Sometimes housing the prisoners involved taking over the state prison as part of the original lease and then sub-contracting the prisoners out to live and work on another site.

This system was most commonly used in the southern states following the Civil War. Before the war there had been no point in imprisoning blacks. As slaves they had no freedom to be deprived of and, in any case, to imprison them would have deprived their white masters of the use of their labour. After the Civil War and the Emancipation Proclamation those blacks who transgressed the law – and many did so in the struggle to scratch a living during a period of severe social and economic disruption – were in an altogether different situation. They were punished with imprisonment and more often than not leased out to contractors to labour on the very land which they had previously worked as slaves. The cruel irony of this new form of penal slavery hardly requires any elaboration.

In a lease situation where the state had relinquished all public responsibility for its prisoners the private contractor was free to make money with little or no regard for the health and well being of those in his charge; this happened in the south on a grand scale. Plantation owners, railway companies and mining corporations all queued up to lease prisoners and work them more or less as slaves which was, in truth, how blacks were still regarded.[40] There were occasional public scandals when, for example, it was reported that leased prisoners were forced to live in disease infested swamps or perhaps when one of their number was beaten to death; but the system stayed in place in some southern states until well into the twentieth century. Why it endured so long has been well summarized by Thorsten Sellin:

> Designed to save taxpayers the expense of supporting prisons and make convict labour a source of revenue it became a windfall for politically powerful leasees who profited from it and therefore opposed its abolition. It was a pernicious system which did nothing to reform offenders and subjected them, temporarily or for life, to a form of chattel slavery even worse than that from which blacks had been freed. It began, grew and flourished only because all those who suffered under it were ex-slaves whom the master class still thought of as belonging to an inferior race. This also accounts for the indifference towards the often shocking neglect and brutality of the base camps, the cause of such abnormally high death and morbidity rates that official investigators in several states concluded that a convict who survived five to seven years in the camps, or two years in some of the lumber camps, could consider himself fortunate.[41]

While the lease system operated in the south and to some extent in the west, the contract system predominated in the north and east. Under this system the state still controlled the prison, fed, clothed and maintained the inmates, but negotiated with an outside contractor to run the prison workshops. The contractor normally paid the state a fixed sum for the prisoner's labour, provided his own raw materials and managed the workshops (and often the distribution of the goods produced) to secure as much profit as he could.[42] A modified version of this practice was the piece-price system in which instead of paying a fixed per capita sum for each prisoner's labour the contractor instead agreed a price for each piece of finished work or article. Under this system the

18

prison staff retained control of the work processes.[43] First introduced into Massachusetts in 1876 this system was obviously seen as second best by private manufacturers and never employed more than around 14 per cent of the workforce.

This transformation of the nineteenth-century North American prison into a factory, which is how Melossi and Pavarini would like us to understand it, came about for a number of reasons.[44] To begin with, and unlike Britain where private manufacturers rarely got much further than the prison gates, America suffered from a shortage of labour. Thus prison industries not only helped to expand production, they also, because prison labour was so shamefully exploited, helped to keep the lid on wages in free society. Apart from manufacturers who made considerable profits, the prison administration also gained. It was estimated by one observer that the contract system could return two-thirds of prison costs whereas the public account system, in which prison officials were totally in control of prison industries, barely covered one-third.

These benefits did not please everyone. Some penal reform groups, for example, argued that the contract between private manufacturers and prisoners could be harmful to the process of reform. Then there were the arguments of those manufacturers who operated outside the prison. They were clearly at a disadvantage cost-wise and demanded curbs on what they saw as unfair competition. Labour organizations also campaigned against unfair competition, arguing that prison labour not only held down wage levels in free society but was also in certain trades a real threat to their members' security of employment. The strength of union opposition is well illustrated by the 1878 milliners' convention which wanted to boycott those who trained prison operatives, remove all manufacturing machinery from prisons and abolish the contract system altogether. As the pace of industrialization picked up in the USA, which it did far later in America than in Britain, the opposition of organized labour turned out to be decisive. Melossi and Pavarini show how private interests, from leaseholders to contractors, were forced out of the prison system:

Protests and agitation in the labour movement against penitentiary production continued right up until 1930, even if the question of competition between the two could be considered as effectively resolved by the end of the century. The official figures around the end of the nineteenth century and the beginning of the twentieth century are significant in this respect. In 1885, for example, 26 per cent of all prisoners employed in productive work were under the leasing system; in 1895, 19 per cent; in 1905, 9 per cent; in 1914, 4 per cent; by 1923, one could consider the system as having been completely done away with. We can see the same thing occurring in relation to the contract system; in 1885, 40 per cent of prisoners worked for private contractors; in 1923, this was down to 12 per cent. There were other, even more important changes: in 1885, 75 per cent of prisoners were employed in productive labour, whilst in 1923, the so-called productive prison population amounted to 61 per cent. This last factor must then be related to the following: the public account system together with the state-use and public-works systems employed just 26 per cent of prison labour in 1885, whilst by 1923 the percentage had risen to 81 per cent.[45]

This victory for organized labour was soon to be reinforced by the law in the shape of federal legislation to regulate inter-state commerce. In 1929 the Hawes–Cooper Act empowered states to prohibit the import of prison-made goods from another state. As if to underline the importance of this measure the Sumner–Ashurst Act in 1940 made it a federal offence for inter-state carriers to transport prison-made goods across state boundaries for private use.[46] At various times after 1900 the federal state also intervened directly by prohibiting the use of prison labour on federal contracts of a specified amount. Limiting the market for prison-made goods in this way rendered prison industries far less attractive to private manufacturers and by the second quarter of the twentieth century, as Melossi and Pavarini's figures show, most prison industries were run by the states themselves producing goods such as licence plates and highway signs for their own use.

The state use system, as it came to be called, was modified to meet the particular economic needs of the south in two ways. First, prison labour was used extensively outside the prison itself on public works such as the construction of roads and bridges. This practice gave rise to the now notorious chain gangs which sometimes led to prisoners being manacled as they slept as well as when they were awake and working.[47] This cruel exploitation of prison labour was strongly condemned between the wars, but continued in use in one form or another in some southern states into the 1950s. The second modification involved states such as Florida and Louisiana where penal farms were set up and run with the same ruthless disregard for human rights as had been shown by the worst of the plantation owners in the years before emancipation.[48]

THE NEW PRISON INDUSTRIES

How do we explain recent attempts to turn back the clock and entice private manufacturers back into the business of exploiting prison labour? One possible explanation is that only private manufacturers can produce enough jobs quickly enough to prevent idle American prisoners in overcrowded prisons from riot and destruction. A second explanation rests on the belief that private manufacturers were, in part at least, forced out of the American prison business by the rise of the rehabilitative ideal which suggested that what prisoners really needed was education and counselling rather than discipline and hard work. Now that this ideal has been discredited private involvement in prison industries is again being sought as the best way of giving enough inmates the kind of job skills which will help them to find regular employment on their release. We do not give great weight to either of these explanations, though both appear either implicitly or explicitly in the report from the National Institute of Justice on *The Privatization of Corrections*. However, we do take seriously the report's argument that prisons are becoming increasingly expensive to run and that in the face of state and federal restraints on public spending prison administrators are looking to make their loss making state industries more profitable, either by managing them more efficiently or by calling in private manufacturers.[49]

The push for greater efficiency is not entirely new. In the mid-1970s the federally funded Law Enforcement Assistance Administration took over a number of prison industries to see if they could be better organized and run for profit. The agency devised a Free Venture model for these industries based around a number of organizing principles such as a full working day, comparable levels of productivity with private industry, the right of industrial managers (and not security staff) to manage and so forth.[50] This model was applied in several states, from Minnesota to South Carolina, and covered a range of enterprises from furniture manufacturing to auto repairs. The programme also encompassed public as well as private enterprises.

The experiment was hardly a resounding success. It was slow to get started and few, if any, of the enterprises ever became fully self-sufficient or profitable. Various explanations of this failure were offered, from the opposition of local trade unions to the difficulties that necessarily face business and industrial managers when trying to operate in a secure environment. It was partly in an attempt to overcome some of these problems and to limit restraints on the free circulation of prison-made goods that the Percy Amendment was passed in 1979. This amendment secured for a handful of states exemption from the laws (as set out above) governing inter-state commerce in prison-manufactured goods. There were a number of safeguards built into the amendment which had to apply to any future experiments: no free worker should lose his or her job as a result of this new trade in inter-state goods; local trade unions had to be consulted; and to soothe both unions and local business interests the going rate for the equivalent job on the outside had to be paid to prisoners. The prisoner could have up to 80 per cent of his or her wages deducted to cover items such as board and restitution payments.[51]

It was hoped that by removing restraints on the free circulation of prison-made goods the Percy Amendment would not only make the state-use industries more profitable but also encourage private manufacturers to renew their interest in the prison as a potential site for investment. This does not seem to have happened. What evidence there is tends to suggest that private interest in prison industries is still fairly modest and even in those states where there is at least some token engagement what typically happens is that private entrepreneurs simply supply the raw materials and some machinery and leave the prison administration to do the rest. For example, the Control Data Corporation set up a computer components assembly line in Stillwater State Prison in Minnesota in 1981, trained the staff and then left the entire operation to the prison authorities, returning only at the end of the process to buy and distribute the product.[52]

But even this degree of arms' length involvement is modest. Private businessmen and manufacturers are in the main staying away. True, there is the much quoted example of Florida; but it is surely a special case which hardly qualifies. Alarmed by a big increase in its correctional budget Florida agreed in 1981 to turn over its prison industries to be run by a private corporation to see if they could be run at a profit. The company (PRIDE) was to be independent from the corrections administration and free to appoint its own managers from the private sector. In 1984 PRIDE finally took over all of Florida's prison industries. However, while PRIDE's progress is so far reported to be encouraging on the costs front, it is insulated from direct competition with the private sector and is in any case a non-profit making corporation. What money it does make goes straight back into the business and not to shareholders.[53] A contrasting example, perhaps, is provided by Zephyr Products Incorporated which is based at Leavenworth, Kansas and run by Harvard business graduate Fred Braun. In this operation 30 inmates are bussed to a factory every day at their own expense. They receive minimum wages out of which they have to pay state charges and also contribute towards the upkeep of their families. However, it is worth noticing that even this much publicized experiment was funded by the local community and made a loss in its first two years.[54]

A list of private firms paying inmates for their services has been compiled by the Commonwealth of Virginia.[55] Here we find, in addition to PRIDE and Zephyr, two separate companies running telephone reservation services from prisons in Arizona and Oklahoma; in Mississippi there is an equipment assembly plant and in Utah a private firm selling correctional industries' products; in Washington 12 companies are apparently involved in manufacturing and services while in Missouri the Moberly Plasma plant is employing up to 30 inmates. Even if this list is not as up-to-date as we might like, or if we have overlooked the odd private initiative here and there, it clearly shows that most prison industries remain firmly in public hands.

It is easy to explain why this should be so. Private manufacturers simply find it difficult to make money out of prison industries, let alone maximize their potential. To begin with there is the constant tension between the security routines of the prison and the requirements of industrial production; disruptive workshop searches are a simple routine necessity and key supervisory staff have to be taken away from production when pressure builds up elsewhere in the system. Also, of course, prisoners are frequently transferred or released and this means new hands have to be trained, often at very short notice. Then there are location costs. As we have observed, prisons are often sited away from cities or the large conurbations where prison goods are likely to be sold. Getting prison goods to the market place can therefore be expensive, pushing up costs and reducing profits.

On top of these very practical difficulties are the legislative obstacles. Eliminating, or at least seriously easing these obstacles, is generally taken to be a pre-condition for the extensive involvement of the private sector in prison industries.[56] It seems improbable, however, that this will happen in the near future, mainly because of opposition from organized labour in the form of the AFL–CIO. Organized labour in America may not be the power it was in the 1960s; but it will not stand idly by and see its members undermined by what it regards as an attempt to introduce slave labour.[57] This is surely at the heart of the matter. It seems to us that Chief Justice Warren's exhortation that America

22

should build 'factories with fences' instead of inhumane 'warehouses' is to translate the past into the present in a very ahistorical manner.[58] Prisons as factories with fences did exist; but they were the product of a particular moment, not just in the development of capitalism *per se*, but more especially in the development of American capitalism.[59] We do not see how the particular set of circumstances which then existed, and this must include the weak state of organized labour, can be repeated. Of course, this does not mean that privately or publicly run prison industries (or a combination of both) do not make money here and there – they clearly do – or that finding constructive work for prisoners is not a good thing, as advocates of privatization, like Hawkins, argue. However, as Robert Weiss has pointed out, the contribution of the private sector in achieving this has not been as benign as some would like to suggest.[60] Nevertheless, we do wish to suggest that the modern prison is neither likely to return as the important site for private entrepreneurial initiatives it once was, nor which some Americans would like it to become. We are, therefore, far less convinced than Auerbach *et al.* that American prisons are about to become an attractive alternative to the 'sometimes expensive move to foreign based production' in countries such as Hong Kong and Korea.[61]

DELIVERING PRISON SERVICES

If there are only modest profits to be made from running prison industries, quite the reverse seems to be true when it comes to delivering prison services; private corporations are clearly active in this market, seeking contracts to provide services such as medical care, catering, staff training and so forth. Those who advocate the extension of this growing practice do so on the following grounds. In the first place they argue that large, specialist corporations can usually provide a better service at a cheaper cost.[62] Take the example of catering. A large corporation might use its market power to buy food in bulk and then prepare some of it away from the prison itself as part of a much larger operation, so reducing unit costs to well below what could be achieved in any conventional prison. Alternatively, the food might be prepared on site using more professional, cost-effective techniques. The professional approach is always emphasized. It is not just, as in the case we have been considering, that corporations can buy big and cheap, but also that they employ people whose business is food (and not corrections). One food corporation took a whole page advertisement in *Corrections Today* to make exactly this point. Accompanying a photograph of its operations in a Chicago jail was the following message:

> Putting together this meal takes more than dishing food on a tray. On this tray line, and lines like it across the country, good meals – over 80,000 daily – are being served three times a day, seven days a week, 52 weeks a year with the same care, quality and control. *This is Szabo performance . . .* the work of tested professionals – *proven managers in the correctional environment.*[63]

23

No irony is intended. Nor indeed, is there any criticism of those public officials who currently prepare and deliver most prison food. The argument, implicit in this case, is simply that general purpose organizations are inherently incapable of delivering high quality, cost-effective specialist services, whether catering, medical or whatever.

The assertion that the private sector can deliver major prison services more efficiently is also accompanied by the more plausible claim that it can also reduce the cost of those services which are used only intermittently. Transport has been given as one example. Prisoners are not transported every day, nor do they come and go on a regular basis in any given week. In these circumstances it might well be cheaper to contract with a local company to provide transport or escort services as and when they are required, rather than hire a full-time driver and maintain a wholly owned prison vehicle. To ensure that the best deal is secured prison administrators are advised to put all contracts to tender, the assumption being that there will be more than one supplier which will generate competition and keep prices down.

It is important to emphasize that the presence of competition is seen as crucial to the cost-effective delivery of other prison services, including medical and catering services. The argument here is that the corporations concerned do not just provide a cheaper and better service in these areas because they are large specialist organizations; they do so mainly because competitors are monitoring their performance, ever willing to undercut and replace them where they can. Conversely, most publicly delivered prison services are expensive and in-efficiently managed, not simply because large general purpose organizations cannot provide specialist managers or buy big in the market place, but because they are, in effect, public monopolies. There is simply no competition and dissatisfied customers can hardly go elsewhere.

It is easy to see why, in theory at least, these arguments appeal to harassed prison administrators working to ever tighter budgets. But what range of services is contracted out? Has the experience of bringing in outside contractors been a successful one? And how much are these contracts worth? Getting answers to these questions is not easy, particularly as the results of the one national survey covering these questions are far from clear. However, it is established that there are a number of services involved. In addition to those already mentioned, for example, some adult institutions also contract out prison maintenance and staff training. While contracts have been cancelled because of poor performance, some prison administrators report satisfaction. So there is movement here and if contracting out can be shown to be truly cost-effective it is possible that other states will follow the example of Minnesota and Louisiana and contract out for food and other services, including rehabilitation. (We mention rehabilitation at this point because the privatization lobby has found some unexpected allies among those who believe that the public's continuing support for rehabilitation offers the opportunity to experiment with privately operated prison reform programmes which, they believe, might turn out to be more successful than those run by public employees.[64]) It is difficult to estimate the overall value of these contracts; but the involvement of companies such as

Correctional Medical Systems (CMS) and Prison Management Services (PMS) as providers of prison medical services suggests their potential.

PRISON MEDICAL SERVICES

The first thing to register about both CMS and PMS is that they are, or have been, subsidiaries of far larger corporations. CMS is a division of Spectrum Emergency Care Incorporated which provides, staffs and manages hospital emergency rooms. Spectrum in its turn is part of ARA Medical Service which is a division of a giant conglomerate valued at several billion dollars. Though smaller and arguably less successful, PMS was still attractive enough to have been taken over by American Medical International, one of the world's largest investor owned hospital corporations.[65] It surely goes without saying that these corporations entered the prison medical market not out of altruism but to make money for their shareholders; they have used the usual range of arguments to promote their services against those of the public sector. Thus PMS claimed to have used America Medical International's nationwide purchasing contracts to buy equipment and supplies at more competitive prices than is open to any local jail or state-wide prison system.[66] Likewise, CMS claims it can provide better professional services. The argument here is that since being a prison physician is regarded as a dead end job, getting any physician is difficult, let alone getting good ones. CMS can allegedly overcome this by plugging into Spectrum's extensive and efficient recruitment network and also by getting better qualified doctors because working for a large corporation offers better career prospects.

These examples sound plausible; but do the results add up to a more effective medical service, including a better service for prisoners? There is certainly some negative evidence. The CMS operation at Reidsville, Georgia is a case in point. Reidsville is interesting because it was subjected to one of the few independent audits of a privately run prison medical contract. The audit was conducted by court-appointed Vincent Nathan. After praising the introduction of policy manuals and the reorganization of medical records at Reidsville, Nathan strongly criticized CMS for its failure to provide continuity in physician assistant coverage. His remarks were based on a supplementary report written by two independent medical experts who also reached the conslusion that CMS had only a 'limited capacity to recruit and retain a well qualified staff'.[67] In fairness, CMS did concede that its service at Reidsville could be improved and later argued that things had been put right. We have no means of testing this claim, but we would suggest that what happened at Reidsville is a necessary antidote to the glossy rhetoric to be found in private medical promotions aimed at correctional administrators.

While the introduction of outside contractors does not always bring the gains that are claimed for it, it is easy to see why, for some prisoners, private medicine may be no worse than the sub-standard public medicine they fought to have outlawed. It is right, of course, that we should support prison struggles to secure better medical services; but the way forward does not necessarily involve aggressive nationwide companies like CMS or PMS, as the example of New York has demonstrated. Following prison disturbances, New York city decided to upgrade its prison medical services. A dual strategy was involved. A first step was to transfer the responsibility for health care from the Department of Corrections to the Health Service Commission and to augment the Commission's resources, including the recruitment of more physicians and nurses. Second, a contract was negotiated with Montefiori Hospital, a local non-profit voluntary institution, to provide a comprehensive range of medical services for the penal complex at Riker's Island. Montefiori was to be responsible for the care of inmates at five institutions, including the Riker's Island infirmary with over 140 beds. The programme was to include a range of services at each institution from screening on reception to emergency care and the provision of several highly specialized services. Montefiori insisted on certain new facilities before it eventually agreed a contract which was valued at around 11.7 billion dollars.[68]

The contract aspect of New York's strategy seems to have worked well and Montefiori has succeeded in overcoming some of the traditional constraints on prison medicine. As an outside agency employing its own professional staff it is not taken to be in direct competition in the sometimes daily struggle for resources (and favours) from the centre. Second, prison medicine is no longer isolated; standards at Riker's Island can be compared with those elsewhere in the city and the necessary resources argued for to keep the two in some sort of balance. There have been problems in recruiting the right calibre of staff in some areas, but the medical service provided by Montefiori is still agreed to be better than elsewhere in New York's prison system. Because hospitals like Montefiori receive no state aid, and because they cannot be supported entirely by donations, they are forced to stay competitive to attract fee paying patients. Combine this with their local base which offers greater accountability and New York's strategy is easy to appreciate. The services provided by Montefiori are not cheap; but as Alabama found out when it decided to go private, a medical service which is considered adequate by the courts can cost a lot, even when it is contracted out to cost conscious companies like PMS and CMS.[69]

Public officials are more than just sceptical about the private sector's ability to provide private medical services more cheaply. Some fear that companies like CMS could all too easily use their professional expertise to oversell the need for their services and so actually *increase* overall costs. The likelihood that competition might guard against such an abuse is fine in theory; but what we actually see among contractors is a tendency towards oligopoly. Absence of competition is likely to be less of a problem at local level where most jails are served by local physicians on a part-time basis.

In spite of these anxieties, contracting out for medical services does appear to be on the increase, partly as a result of court orders forcing state and local authorities to improve their services and partly as a result of work by the American Correctional Association in alliance with public health authorities and the medical profession to set basic prison health standards. In its *Report on Private Sector Involvement in Prison Service Operations* in 1984 the National

Institute of Corrections published a nationwide survey showing that contracting for physicians' services, health services and medical health services were the most frequently used contract services.[70] Private sector involvement in prison medicine is minimal in Britain, where the state controls the prison medical service from the centre and where supporting services come mainly from the socialized health service to which everyone contributes. This could change if the provision of private medical care continues to grow.

Private medicine in America is not confined to the deep end of the penal system. This is particularly so if we go beyond the medical treatment of routine physical disease to include drug or substance abuse and mental health. As a condition of probation an offender might agree to attend a treatment centre for drug or substance addiction and that centre could well be run privately and for profit. Valle Management Associates, for example, claim to design, implement and then run substance abuse programmes for courts, as well as for jails and prisons.[71] In many states a good deal of mental health care is dressed up as counselling in one form or another and delivered by profit making private agencies in various community settings from halfway houses for adults to secure homes for juveniles. As in the case of the treatment centres mentioned above, public authorities in these circumstances contract out where they can an agreed programme on a competitive basis. Monitoring the quality and efficiency of these programmes is seen to be a problem. However, what concerns some critics of these privately operated community programmes is not their efficiency, or even that they operate for profit, but more that their proliferation represents an unwelcome extension of the state's power to punish. This is an important line of argument to which we will return; but for the moment let us look more closely at the variety of private interests at work in this, the shallow end of the American penal system.

THE SHALLOW END

Building (or converting) and then running penal institutions for profit is by no means unusual in this part of the system. A reasonable proportion of all halfway houses, for example, are run as profit making enterprises. Although by no means a wholly new penal initiative – they existed in one form or another in the nineteenth century – the rapid growth of halfway houses in America was a notable feature of the 1960s and 1970s. This expansion can best be explained in two ways. To begin with, it reflected a loss of faith in the rehabilitative ideal. Keeping offenders out of prison, or getting those who were already in prison out as soon as possible, was the main aim of most penal reform groups during this period and halfway houses were seen as one means of achieving this goal, particularly from the second half of the 1960s. Second, as prison populations rose so providing alternatives to custody came to be seen as a political necessity to relieve overcrowding and reduce costs. Re-enter pragmatism. The extent of the expansion triggered off by these concerns was reflected in the growth of the American-based International Halfway House Association. Whereas in 1964 it consisted of around 30 agencies, its reported membership in 1974 was closer to 2,500.[72] That there was a profit to be made out of this expansion did not pass unnoticed and some of the Association's members clearly saw it as a legitimate business opportunity. A survey by the National Institute of Justice published in 1985 found that non-secure community facilities for adults, including halfway houses, were under private contract in 32 states, though no estimate was made of how many of these were run by profit making organizations.[73]

Most of the profit making activity in America is probably concentrated in the juvenile sector, where recreationally orientated, community-based projects for young offenders, or would-be offenders, proliferated from the late 1960s onwards. The burgeoning of these programmes is partly explained by the growing conviction that incarcerating children is not only even more expensive than incarcerating adults but is equally ineffective in turning them away from crime. Alternatives therefore have to be found and while voluntary, non-profit agencies have certainly delivered their share of community programmes to run alongside those offered by the state, profit making companies like Vision Quest also moved into the market.

Vision Quest's programme is based on extensive 'wilderness training' which appears to be similar, at least in spirit, to what we in Britain would identify as the training offered by Outward Bound. Activities vary from mountain climbing and long hikes to the well publicized wagon trains which travel hundreds of miles around the country and last for several weeks. Youngsters are confronted – by situations and counsellors – throughout their training and in the course of their activities learn a good deal about themselves and their strengths as well as their weaknesses – or at least that is the theory. While some accuse Vision Quest of mass intimidation, others believe that its tough physical programme is just what difficult children need.[74] Where the truth lies between these conflicting assessments is difficult to judge, especially at a distance. However, one thing is clear; the programme has been good for business. Vision Quest was reported at one time to have an annual budget running into millions of dollars, to employ a staff of over 250 and to make a very reasonable return for its three major stockholders. What Vision Quest has done for profit on a grand scale plenty of others do on a small scale.

It would be quite wrong to give the impression that privatization at what we have somewhat loosely described as the shallow end of the system is confined only to the provision of alternatives to custody. On the contrary, the recent report of the President's Commission on privatization is quick to point out that two-thirds of America's 3,000, mainly low security, juvenile detention and correctional institutions were in private hands.[75] These private facilities clearly play an important part in the American juvenile justice system and while their reported numerical explosion in the 1970s was probably exaggerated, there now seems little doubt that as a result of changes in federal funding from the early 1960s they played a significant part in widening the net at that part of the system where the boundary between control and welfare becomes blurred and where correctional and welfare departments overlap in their struggle to secure resources.[76] However, what we do not know, and what the report of the

President's Commission on privatization could not tell us because of the way in which the United States Bureau of Census compiles its statistics, is just how many of these institutions were profit making organizations and what their overall financial strength might amount to.[77] The only marginally useful estimate we are aware of was made in 1984 by the National Institute of Corrections in its report on *Private Sector Involvement in Prison Services and Operations*, when it estimated that the overall cost of such services and operations was about 200 million dollars and that two-thirds of this figure was spent by juvenile agencies.[78] But again, exactly how much of this very considerable sum was consumed by profit making agencies is not recorded.

PRIVATIZATION AND COMMODIFICATION

To contextualize and better understand some of these developments it is helpful to remind ourselves that at about the same time as reform groups first began to seriously challenge the efficacy of prisons the federal government was already taking on a more positive role in helping a whole range of disadvantaged groups, a policy which had been forced on President Johnson as the impetus of civil rights agitation spread from the south into the northern black ghettoes.[79] But in the absence of well developed central and local agencies to deliver that help – as exist in Britain's unitary welfare state – the federal government turned to a whole range of voluntary and non-voluntary groups during the Great Society era – as it came to be called – to deliver its aid.[80] True, this aid was often channelled through state and local governments or through newly created federal agencies; but very often the delivery service was left to a mushrooming number of local groups, some of which were voluntary and non-profit making and others of which were not. It was in the context of this decentralized and loosely structured welfare service that the late 1960s and early 1970s delivery of punishment took place.

This was an opportunity which different groups used in different ways. Some groups merely extended their long standing, voluntary commitment to help those being punished; others simply used it as a means to make money out of operating halfway houses or whatever. Still others, notably those associated with the New Left, sought to break out of the dovetailing of public welfare with profit making concerns which so characterizes American monopoly capitalism by mobilizing the disadvantaged as a political force.[81] Offenders were seen as being not only victims of an unjust criminal justice system, but also as part of a wider community-based alliance of oppressed groups operating outside the formal political apparatus of the state, with the potential for fighting for radical social and political change which the traditional working class could not be relied upon to deliver. While similar opportunities (and aspirations) could be said to have existed in Britain and reasonably successful attempts were made to mobilize welfare recipients and other groups, and to secure government aid to build alternative centres of power in the teeth of the great Leviathan, non-governmental groups operating in and around the penal system never had anything like the same potential for leverage on the centralized welfare state as

29

in America, whether they were fomenting political opposition or simply trying to make a 'fast buck'. But we will return to these initiatives later.

In the meantime, however, it must be remembered that the political ascendancy of the New Right in the USA led to a drastic cut in the number of federal government initiatives in the provision of welfare and human services and resources are now relatively more scarce than in the past. This is not to suggest that private organizations are no longer a significant force in America. On the contrary, one estimate suggests that non-profit and profit making private organizations together still deliver over 60 per cent of all welfare or human services in the USA. The non-profit sector alone employs six and a half million people and accounts for about 5 per cent of America's gross national product.[82] However, what tighter funding at federal (and state) levels has led to is the further commodification of welfare and human services and the adoption of aggressive business practices by non-profit and profit making organizations alike. In their desperate attempts to attract funds, to ensure that it is their bid which succeeds, private organizations of both kinds have slimmed down their operations to make them more cost-effective. They have actively sought out new clients whom they hope will attract grants because they are seen by those in authority as more 'legitimate' and therefore more deserving and have increasingly gone on to market their clients as *commodities* rather than to assert or advocate their welfare and human *rights*.[83] Securing help in such hard times for those with a low legitimacy ranking – adult offenders and ex-offenders being a case in point – is not easy and opportunities for the sort of politically radical work undertaken in the 1960s and 1970s are severely restricted. Because of this the experience of those being processed by the private sector in America may be much the same in both non-profit and profit making organizations.

Evidence of the pressure on voluntary organizations throughout America either to go out and 'really compete' for funds and/or turn what were conceived of as social programmes into businesses has been provided by Lynn Curtis in his report on three neighbourhood projects involving offenders in New York (Argus), Ponce (El Centro) and Philadelphia (Umoja). While the initiative for each of these projects came from very different sources, all have been successful in operating around the principle of an extended social family based on strict rules and training for employment. Though much praised for their innovative methods, all three projects feel under great pressure to become more aggressive in marketing their organizations or to make money in areas which are hardly entrepreneurial paradises:

> Argus, El Centro and Umoja are aware of the rhetoric of the times – that community organisations need to become more 'financially self-sufficient', particularly by learning to become more sophisticated fund raisers in a traditional sense, as well as by striving to transform some activities from social programmes to profit-making businesses. But this is not easy to do, especially in the markets available in low income communities and given the scarcity of start-up capital for what private public sources alike view as high risk ventures.[84]

It seems clear that in its retreat from the Great Society era the American state is now even less inclined to treat those in need as citizens with rights and needs which it has a duty to secure and protect, both prompted and assisted by the voluntary sector. Instead, welfare in its various forms is now regarded more and more as a commodity to be somehow traded in the market place by cost conscious organizations which sometimes seem more interested in securing the next bid than looking to the welfare of their clients, let alone trying to give them political clout. While some in Britain have toyed with the idea of going some way towards this system, it seems to us very undesirable indeed.[85]

EXTENT AND OPPOSITION

There is certainly more to be discovered about the American experience of privatization. For example, our research could unearth little on the operation of a facility for parole violators in California, or the women's prison run by the Volunteers of America at Roseville. The Volunteers have twice refused requests for information about their operation; but from scattered press reports we gather that they are out only to cover their costs and have provided a better than usual physical environment. On the other hand, to describe Roseville's facilities as like those found in a Holiday Inn is to ignore the fact that women prisoners are stripped searched and subject in other ways to standard prison discipline, including solitary confinement.[86] It is important to have a fuller account of what happens at Roseville since women's prisons are particularly vulnerable to privatization, being seen as marginal and suitable to be hived off. This is because they are relatively few and the women are perceived as a low risk category with special medical and welfare needs.

Apart from these obvious gaps in our knowledge we are none the less confident enough about our survey to suggest that the American experience of privatizing the delivery of punishment overall is both uneven and limited. It is uneven in that it is more prevalent in the south, where fiscal conservatism is strong and where unions are weak, than in the north; more common in the juvenile sector than in adult corrections; more likely to apply to service delivery than to the ownership and/or management of whole facilities; even when it comes to raising capital for new prisons or jails, there is no uniform practice. And it is limited in the sense that privatization has had only a modest impact on the American penal system as a whole. Granted, there are important exceptions to this, in the juvenile sector and at the shallow end of the adult system; but our impression is that much of what passes for privatization in these contexts, though significant and arguably worrying in ways, is confined to non-profit making agencies – though we acknowledge that we are unable to put an exact figure on the balance between profit and non-profit making involvement in this part of the system.

The limited progress of profit making corporations in the American correctional system is partly explained by the fact that a wide range of pressure groups have mobilized to fight it – groups which in many ways have very little in common. Among the first groups to voice their opposition was the National Sheriffs' Association. As we saw in Chapter 1, elected sheriffs are largely responsible for running local and county jails and they feel both aggrieved and threatened by privatization for several reasons. To start with, the state of many local jails has rendered them subject to court order and while those sheriffs directly concerned must take their fair share of the blame, their case is that the main fault lies with elected politicians who have consistently failed to provide the necessary cash for improvements, preferring instead to spend money on local schools, roads and hospitals. But what is worse, argue the sheriffs, having neglected jails to the point where there is now widespread overcrowding and a shortage of trained personnel, local politicians are planning to turn them over to the private sector to put things right – if they can – on the cheap. Apart from their anger at this attempt to 'pass the buck', sheriffs are also anxious that whereas those who now run prisons are publicly accountable through the ballot box, private contractors would be shielded from any direct form of accountability and therefore less likely to maintain standards or, where necessary, argue for improvements, especially if these might endanger their contracts.[87] Furthermore, and this should come as no surprise, the sheriffs believe that the reluctance of local politicians to provide adequate funding, and the need for private contractors to make a profit, will lead not only to an overall reduction in staffing levels, but also to the recruitment of less qualified personnel to do what they maintain is a difficult and demanding job.

For all these reasons, and as far back as June 1984, the Sheriffs' Association passed a resolution at its annual conference opposing privatization. This opposition was publicly re-stated following its participation at a forum on corrections and the private sector sponsored by the National Institute of Justice in February 1985:

> For the past fifteen years, the National Sheriffs' Association has passed a significant amount of time, resources and energy devoted to helping sheriffs improve their jail operations. . . . We believe that the sheriffs and their jail staffs have done a commendable job under less than desirable circumstances. *We are unalterably opposed to taking jails away from sheriffs and turning them over to private organizations.* We feel that the counties and the states in cooperation with elected sheriffs should devote much more effort to professionalizing the jail operation. Only when this commitment is made will the jail problem begin to subside [our emphasis].[88]

Another group whose members feel threatened by privatization is the American Federation of State, County and Municipal Employees (AFSCME). Something like 40,000 of its 1.4 million members are directly involved in corrections and the Federation has vigorously opposed privatization by drawing on its long experience in other areas. It has pointed out that in the early years of the present century many American cities and towns contracted out a whole range of public services; but problems were frequent. Contractors often over-charged, gave poor service and in some service areas and in some cities corruption was endemic. In an attempt to stamp on these abuses the local government reform movement in the 1920s successfully argued for the return of many of these services to the public sector. The Federation believes that contracting out correction is likely to lead to similar abuses and during the Reagan years, which have seen a plethora of scandals involving public figures at all levels of government, it is difficult not to take this anxiety seriously.[89] To be sure, this genuine concern for the integrity of public sector services, like the sheriff's emphasis on professionalism, should not hide the simple fact that what concerns both groups most is the likelihood that privatization will lead to a loss of jobs for their members and poorer conditions of service for those who are kept on. We, and they, use the term 'likelihood' since the main selling point of most forms of privatization is that outside contractors can deliver correctional services more cheaply than hitherto and given that the corrections industry is labour-intensive, it seems reasonable to assume that a good proportion of any savings will come from hiring fewer staff or perhaps by paying the staff who remain less money or reduced pensions. At Okeechobee this has already happened.[90]

Apart from its apparent willingness to fight against any cuts, the Federation also commissioned a legal publicist to argue against those private sector interests who identify overpaid and restrictive public sector unions as being an impediment to progress and efficiency. For J. Michael Keating, on behalf of the Federation, such a strong anti-union posture is easy to attack. He writes:

> While the rhetoric of private entrepreneurs is rich with lamentations about the direct and indirect costs of correctional unions, there is little corresponding understanding of the benefits derived from regularized relations between management and labour in correctional institutions. Once a prison or jail is built, the business of corrections is highly labor-intensive; the provision of 24 hour, seven days a week supervision of prisoners is what makes correctional institutions so expensive to operate. In terms of salary, benefits, training and respect and recognition, correctional officers have always been at the bottom of the criminal justice heap. Because the job pays so poorly, hiring standards are low; because training is minimal, new recruits learn their jobs through trial and error; because they are ill equipped and ill trained to perform their duties, burn-out and turn-over rates are phenomenal; because economy so often requires a reduction in the ratio of staff to prisoners, supervision of inmates is often inadequate and violence flourishes; because the pressure and violence of the institutional environment generate incredible stress, absenteeism is high, overtime is rampant and operational costs tend to skyrocket. Every major commission and study group that has looked at corrections in the past two decades has emphasized the need for selective recruitment, higher salaries, much more training . . . all have bemoaned the impact of high turnover on correctional efficiency. It is precisely these issues that unions have addressed most effectively in corrections. In unionized states and localities, recruitment tends to be more selective, salaries and benefits are higher,

more training is provided, more staff is available and turnover is much reduced. Given the labor intensity of corrections any substantial reduction in the rate of turnover is a tremendous boost to productivity.[91]

Keating's contribution has been made widely available and helps to illustrate how yet another public sector union opposed to privatization is up and running and putting forward a cogent case in defence of its own interests.

Keating also touches on the thorny question of costs.[92] The evidence about costs is very sketchy indeed and we take the view that there is, as yet, no reliable evidence to suggest that the private operation of entire facilities will be more cost-effective than if the same or comparable facilities were to be run by public agencies. On this particular judgement we are in agreement with the report of the President's Commission on privatization and the Legislative Research Council of the Commonwealth of Massachusetts, both of which, significantly, came out in *favour* of privatization.[93] Granted, it is possible to find cases here and there where savings seem to have been secured. After earlier cost overruns, for example, it is now claimed that modest savings are being made at Silverdale, though this conclusion is highly tentative; and we referred earlier to the use by the INS of privately owned and run detention centres for illegal immigrants.[94] These reduced costs to the federal government of around 6 per cent arose mainly because the contractors paid lower wages and benefits than the government.[95] On the other hand, the state authorities in Kentucky believe that they get no real savings from the private operation of Saint Mary Prison. The issue of costs, then, is far from settled, and this uncertainty is taken by the unions (and others) to be a major weakness in the case of those who argue for privatization. Another perceived weakness is that some of the leading proponents of privatization, figures such as Don Hutto (CCA) and Alan Ault (Justice Systems Incorporated), were formerly in charge of state prisons which were either under court order or found to be unconstitutional. This far from encouraging record has led critics like Keating to doubt the ability of private entrepreneurs to achieve, with even fewer resources, what they so manifestly failed to achieve as public employees.[96] But turning now from trade union worries, what about the status and rights of prisoners in privately operated prisons?

CIVIL RIGHTS

Unlike Britain, the United States has a written constitution and a Bill of Rights and these provisions have helped prisoners to safeguard their rights and improve their living conditions by appealing to the courts. One of the most active pressure groups in this field is the National Prison Project which operates under the auspices of the American Civil Liberties Union (ACLU). Although by no means a natural ally of the Sheriffs' Association, the Project has nevertheless lined up with the sheriffs in their opposition to privatizing prisons and jails. In September 1986 the following resolution was passed by the Project's steering committee and recommended to the ACLU:

The delegation of control and custody of prisoners to private entities, in and of itself, raises serious constitutional concerns. Because the deprivation of freedom is one of the most severe interferences with liberty the state can impose, and because of the civil liberties concerns created by private management, some of which are listed below, the power to deprive another of his/her freedom cannot be delegated to private entities. The civil liberties concerns, because of the history of abuse, include the following;

1. Prisoners are likely to suffer deprivation because of placement in a private prison.
2. Private prisons are likely to have an adverse impact on various aspects of a prisoner's life or on the factors that affect the duration of his/her confinement.
3. Private prisons are likely to have an adverse impact on substantive and procedural legal rights and remedies of prisoners.
4. It is likely that a private prison will not comply with all the relevant health and safety standards.
5. Private prisons are likely to result in inappropriate confinement or an inappropriate use of incarceration as a sanction.
6. While meaningful work opportunities are both necessary and appropriate, private management is likely to cause exploitation of prisoners under poor working conditions without remuneration for the financial benefit of the private entity.[97]

There is a whole range of issues (and worries) covered by points 1 and 2. For example, in many states prisoners can earn what is called 'good time'. This is the equivalent of what we in Britain call 'remission'. The decision to grant 'good time' is dependent on the behaviour of the prisoner as reported by staff. In a privately run prison the decision – and remember it is a decision about whether or not to grant a person his or her freedom – would be taken by a private citizen and, what is more, by a citizen whose financial interest might well be directly served by denying 'good time'. Such a situation is thought to be open to abuse.

There are similar problems surrounding parole. Being granted parole is a far more complex process, but part of that process is an assessment by staff of the prisoner's behaviour and in a private prison this assessment would again be made by someone with a direct pecuniary interest. To argue that this assessment would have to be made according to strict rules which have been drawn up by the state is thought simply to beg the question. What applies to parole, also applies to discipline. Inmates break prison rules all the time; in such a tightly regulated setting it is difficult to do otherwise. Sometimes prisoners are allowed to 'get away with it', at other times they are brought before the warden and disciplined. The question now being raised by the National Prison Project (and others) is, should society delegate to a private citizen the exercise of this discretion which is, in effect, the power to punish? It is apparently already difficult enough to safeguard prisoners' rights in all these crucial areas as it is, because while the courts have been prepared to declare whole prison systems unconstitutional under the Eighth Amendment on grounds of inhumane conditions or treatment, as we have seen, they have taken a decidedly 'hands off' approach to what are seen as day to day prison routines, including decisions about discipline and early release, largely deferring in these matters instead to the correctional officer's expertise.[98] That private operators might make improper use of this judicial deference is a genuine anxiety. Another worry in this context, though by no means the most pressing one, is the possibility that privately run prisons might be tempted to use disciplinary procedures to remove difficult inmates to public prisons and leave themselves with the easy cases (Americans refer to this process as skimming).

To be fair, some of these questions worry the advocates of privatization and not just the National Prison Project. So, for example, there has been the suggestion that decisions about 'good time' and parole might be taken by on-site state employees.[99] It is difficult for opponents of privatization to be convinced by such safeguards, however, since it is far from clear how they could be made to work in practice, to say nothing of what they might add to the running costs of a private prison. On this highly sensitive issue there is surely something to be said for the frankness of the pro-privatization report of the Massachusetts Legislative Research Council which admitted that on issues such as discipline it was probably impossible to eliminate private employee involvement.[100] The same report was also disarmingly open about the use of non-deadly force. Private contractors would simply have to be authorized to use non-deadly force in a wide range of circumstances, from trying to prevent an escape to simply making an unwilling prisoner move on. As for the use of deadly force, the report felt that it should be used as a last resort and then only to prevent death, serious bodily injury or if necessary to prevent an escape.[101] Privately employed prison guards, even if they are dressed in casual clothes rather than uniforms and refer to prisoners as residents rather than inmates, are likely to be given this awesome power.

At this point it is surely obvious why the ACLU has become involved in the politics of privatization and why the more conservative American Bar Association has cautioned that jurisdictions considering the privatization of prisons and jails should, 'not proceed to contract until the complex, constitutional, statutory and contractual issues are satisfactorily developed and resolved'.[102] The Association is particularly concerned with what it terms the 'symbolic issue' and its practical consequences. The argument here is that to give up to the private sector what is traditionally taken to be a state function could seriously undermine the legitimacy and authority of those exercising that function, a serious concern which it has posed somewhat ironically by asking, 'Does it weaken that authority, however – as well as the integrity of a system of *justice* – when an inmate looks at his keeper's uniform and, instead of encountering an emblem that reads "Federal Bureau of Prisons" or "State Department of Corrections", he faces one that says "Acme Corrections Company"?'[103]

Given this legal caution it is surprising that the American Correctional Association, which represents something like 40,000 'correctional professionals' should be so openly in favour of privatization. It argues that there is nothing wrong with the use of profit making organizations to fund, build and operate prisons when such use is both cost-effective and 'consistent with the public interest'.[104] The problem with such a position is, of course, that it leaves the all important debate about what constitutes the public interest to others and many of the awkward questions raised by the Project simply go begging. It is not insignificant that the Association, with its role in accrediting standards, finds itself a legitimate target for a complex network of construction, security and other business interests, as a casual glance at *Corrections Today* will show. (The Corrections Corporation of America's executive vice-president, Don Hutto, is a former vice-president of the American Correctional Association.[105])

We interpret point 5 of the Project's statement to explain why some reform groups in the USA are so opposed to privatizing the delivery of punishment, even if their literature is sometimes thin or evasive when it comes to criticizing the profit motive. What we mean by this is that for some groups in the penal lobby too many Americans are being imprisoned as it is and privatization is likely to increase this number. What is required, therefore, is not a policy geared towards expanding the penal system, which is what privatization is all about, but rather a policy geared towards keeping offenders out of prison altogether. Thus, what we take to be a fairly typical response to privatizing punishment is well illustrated by Russ Immarigeon, a former research associate for the Unitarian-sponsored National Moratorium on Prison Construction. He writes that 'the private financing of jails and prison construction is primarily harmful because it encourages rather than restricts the expanded use of imprisonment'.[106] In other words, the profit making nature of these proposals may be troublesome, perhaps; but it is more injurious that they actively promote existing public policies of the overuse and expansion of imprisonment. Entrepreneurial interest *per se* is not the main issue. We take the logic of this argument to be that pre-trial reports – social enquiry reports in British terms – conducted by profit making agencies, something which is already being tried in the USA, would be tolerable, provided that it could be shown that their use led to fewer prison sentences.[107]

Given America's federal system and the right of each state to decide for itself whether or not it wishes to privatize the delivery of punishment, most oppositional alliances have been put together at local level. So, for example, in Tennessee the state's Civil Liberties Union, the American Federation of State, County and Municipal Employees (AFSCME) and local prison reform activists fought CCA's attempt to take over the whole of the state's penal system.[108] The campaign against privatization in Pennsylvania was a particularly fierce one and was mobilized against Buckingham Security's plan to build a prison for those in protective custody. A Bill empowering the state to negotiate an annual fee, set standards and monitor the progress of the new prison was drawn up and introduced into the legislative assembly. This saw the start of a frantic period of lobbying and coalition building on all sides. Those who opposed the Bill formed a broadly based local Coalition for a Moratorium on Private Prisons which included the state AFL–CIO organization, the Pennsylvania Council of Churches, the Urban Coalition and the Guardian Civic League and a black police officers' organization. With the backing of nationwide organizations like the

ACLU and the American Federation of State, County and Municipal Employees, the local coalition succeeded in defeating the Bill and passed its own measure to block any further attempts at privatization pending more research and enquiry.[109]

CONCLUSION

We should make it clear that the broadly based opposition we have been describing is directed mainly at the private construction and management of adult prisons and jails for profit. True, AFSCME fears that any growth in the private delivery of prison services will by definition cost its members and is therefore campaigning on this front too; there is also opposition in some quarters to raising money for new prisons by sidestepping local referenda, which is taken to be an expensive, inappropriate and undemocratic way of handling America's penal crisis; and there are also those who caution against the over-zealous use of privately constructed cellular units. But none of these developments is opposed with the same vigour, or succeeds in uniting as many interests, as the private construction and management of adult prisons and jails. While this is perfectly understandable – some of the issues privatization raises in this case are surely fundamental – it is perhaps surprising that few of these issues feature prominently in articles on those privately run, profit making, juvenile institutions and adult halfway houses which operate at the shallow end of the system.

What all this suggests to us is that those who oppose privatizing the delivery of punishment will need to be vigilant. The American prison business, as Jessica Mitford once described it, remains a potentially lucrative market and private entrepreneurs are unlikely to ignore it because they have been outmanoeuvred in a few localities. Moreover, there is still political pressure for privatization from the centre. For example, the report of the President's Commission on privatization has called for more research on the issue and this has been translated into a budget request currently before the American Congress for:

> three new institutions to be constructed with private sector financing, and then leased, staffed and operated by the Bureau of Prisons, a request for contracting for the total operation and management of one new minimum security institution and the establishment of a privately operated prison industry.[110]

While it is true that having so far secured few benefits from privatization, the Bureau of Prisons is hardly enthusiastic about this federal initiative, the experiment will obviously go ahead if Congress agrees.[111] Of course, Congressional approval cannot be taken for granted given the American budgetary process and it may be significant that President George Bush is noticeably less strident in his privatization rhetoric than was President Reagan. But even if political pressure from the centre were to wane, the federal structure of American government leaves plenty of room for manoeuvre at state and local levels, as we have already demonstrated, and while the current war against drugs encourages more and more offenders to be sent to prison and state and local politicians continue to believe that they are bereft of realistic alternative options, then prison overcrowding will continue and privatization will stay on the agenda. Thus, while we repeat our earlier assessment that overall the American experience of making money out of punishment is so far uneven and limited, especially at the deep end of the system, the debate about what that experience has amounted to, and whether it should be extended, is still very much alive.

We accept that this report on the American experience is neither as exhaustive as it could be nor entirely objective. Quite apart from the fact that we doubt that any investigation along the lines we have conducted could ever be value free, we came to the idea of privatizing the delivery of punishment with certain anxieties and reservations. We feel it is important to be open about this. On the other hand, we would like to believe that our investigation has been more thorough and more objective than most other enquiries undertaken in Britain, particularly by those who would like us to borrow from the American experience. It is to this debate that we now turn.

NOTES

1. J. G. Fox, 'Conservative social policy, social control and racism: the politics of New York State prison expansion, 1975–1985', in B. Rolston and M. Tomlinson (eds), *The Expansion of European Prison Systems*, EDC, Belfast, 1986.
2. *Ibid.*, *passim.*
3. *Ibid.*, pp. 102–3. For another view of this controversy see J. B. Jacobs and J. Berkowitz, 'Reflections on the defeat of the New York State's prison bond', in J. B. Jacobs (ed.), *New Perspectives on Prison and Imprisonment*, Cornell University Press, Ithaca, 1983.
4. It is important to point out that local government in Britain does raise its own finance for other capital projects, such as public housing and leisure centres. For a view of this ever changing scene, see T. Travers, *The Politics of Local Government Finance*, Allen and Unwin, London, 1986.
5. National Institute of Justice, *The Privatization of Corrections*, Washington, DC, 1985, Chapter 3.
6. For general details of local and state finances, see R. A. Musgrave and P. B. Musgrave, *Public Finances in Theory and Practice*, McGraw Hill, London and New York, 1984.
7. Large losses incurred in the 1987 stock market crash led to the merger of Shearson Lehman and E. F. Hutton to become Shearson Lehman, Hutton.
8. *Op. cit.*, note 5, Chapter 3.
9. Between 1983 and 1985 Shearson Lehman/American Express was reported to have raised over 500 million dollars in prison finance, but we cannot be sure whether all of this was used to underwrite new prison building or for other purposes and this figure therefore needs to be used cautiously in the present context. See R. Weiss, 'Private prisons and the state', in R. Matthews (ed.), *Privatizing Criminal Justice*, Sage, London, forthcoming.

10. *Op. cit.*, note 5, p. 43.
11. *Ibid.*, pp. 47–8.
12. See, for example, *Privatization in Corrections*, Commonwealth of Virginia, 1986, p. 38 and C. Mayer, 'Legal issues surrounding private operation of prisons', *Criminal Law Bulletin*, 22, 4, 1986.
13. *Op. cit.*, note 5, p. 67. C. H. Logan and S. A. Rausch also list a privately financed and operated prison in Palo Duro used by the Federal Bureau of Prisons for immigrants convicted of criminal offences; 'Punishment and profit: the emergence of private enterprise prisons', *Justice Quarterly*, 2, 3, 1985. However, the Bureau claims no current knowledge of this facility (Bartolo personal communication).
14. *Op. cit.*, note 12, Commonwealth of Virginia, pp. 70–71.
15. *Ibid.*, p. 79.
16. *Op. cit.*, note 5, p. 59.
17. *The Progressive*, March 1984.
18. *Op. cit.*, note 12, Commonwealth of Virginia, p. 79.
19. The riot later spread to the Atlanta federal penitentiary.
20. Legislative Research Council, The Commonwealth of Massachusetts, *Prisons for Profit*, p. 89. In case law, *Medina* v. *O'Neill*.
21. *Op. cit.*, note 12, Mayer and also the evidence of Ira Robbins before the US House of Representatives. *Subcommittee on Courts, Civil Liberties and the Administration of Justice of the Committee of the Judiciary, Ninety-ninth Congress, First and Second Sessions on Privatization of Corrections, November 1985, March 1986*, Washington, DC, US Government Printing Office, 1968.
22. See, for example, Don Hutto's evidence before the US Senate. *District of Columbia, Subcommittee of the Committee of Appropriations, Ninety-ninth Congress, First Session on RH 3067, An Act Making Appropriations for the Government of the District of Columbia*, Washington, DC, US Government Printing Office, 1985. For a legal perspective on indemnity see Ira Robbins, *The Legal Dimensions of Private Incarceration*, American Bar Association, Washington, DC, 1988.
23. C. R. Ring, *Contracting for the Operation of Private Prisons*, American Correctional Association, Maryland, 1987, p. 36.
24. For the legal arguments surrounding this delegation of the power to punish see *op. cit.*, note 12, Mayer.
25. *Op. cit.*, note 12, Commonwealth of Virginia, pp. 57 and 60.
26. Gilbert Geis, 'The privatization of prisons: panacea or placebo?', in B. J. Carroll, R. W. Conant and T. A. Easton (eds), *Private Means, Public Ends*, Praeger, New York, 1987.
27. Ring, p. 4. *Op. cit.*, note 23, p. 4.
28. J. M. Keating, *Seeking Profit in Punishment: The Private Management of Correctional Institutions*, American Federation of State, County and Municipal Employees, Washington, DC, 1986, p. 15.
29. A. Smith, 'A person, not a number', *Newsweek*, 29 June 1987.
30. See K. Krajick, *Prisons for Profit: The Private Alternative*, State Legislature, April 1984.
31. National Institute of Corrections, *Private Sector Operation of a Correctional Institution*, Washington, DC, 1983.
32. *Ibid.*, p. 16.
33. *Ibid.*, p. 73.
34. *Ibid.*, p. xiii.

35. National Institute of Justice, *Contracting for the Operation of Prisons and Jails*, Washington, DC, 1987.

36. C. H. Logan, 'Proprietary prisons', in L. Goodstein and D. Mackenzie (eds), *The American Prison: Issues in Research and Policy*, Plenum, New York, forthcoming. A larger number of juveniles are held in non-secure institutions, see p. 28.

37. D. K. Sechrest, N. Pappas and S. J. Price, 'Building prisons: pre-manufactured, pre-fabricated and prototype', *Federal Probation*, March 1987.

38. For an assessment of this expanding market see *op. cit.*, note 12, Commonwealth of Virginia, p. 48.

39. Funke *et al.*, *Assets and Liabilities of Correctional Industries*, Lexington Books, Lexington, 1982, pp. 10–12.

40. For the plight of the minority of white prisoners caught up in the lease system, see J. T. Sellin, *Slavery and the Penal System*, Elsevier, New York, 1976, Chapter 11.

41. *Ibid.*, pp. 161 and 162.

42. *Op. cit.*, note 39, pp. 9–10.

43. *Ibid.*, p. 11.

44. D. Melossi and M. Pavarini, *The Prison and the Factory*, Macmillan/Società editrice il Mulino, London/Bologna, 1981.

45. *Ibid.*, p. 141.

46. B. Auerbach, 'New prison industries legislation: the private sector re-enters the field', *Prison Journal*, autumn/winter 1982, 62, p. 26.

47. *Op. cit.*, note 40, pp. 166 and 167.

48. *Ibid.*, pp. 170 ff.

49. *Op. cit.*, note 5, pp. 11–12.

50. *Ibid.*, pp. 12–13.

51. *Op. cit.*, note 46, p. 27.

52. *Op. cit.*, note 5, p. 21.

53. *Ibid.*, p. 22. We have recently discovered that like Florida, Oregon has also handed over its entire prison works programme to private sector managers, but as yet we have been unable to find out on what commercial basis the new enterprise operates.

54. *Ibid.*, pp. 23–24. The best that the National Institute of Justice can say about this and other private sector experiments is that it is too early to say whether they have succeeded or failed. National Institute of Justice, *Private Sector Involvement in Prison-Based Industries* (1985), p. 82.

55. *Op. cit.*, note 12, Commonwealth of Virginia, p. 68.

56. *Op. cit.*, note 5, p. 24.

57. *Ibid.*, p. 24.

58. *Ibid.*, p. 11.

59. For more on the factory as a disciplinary apparatus rather than simply as a unit of production, see for example, M. Foucault, *Discipline and Punish*, Allen Lane, London, 1977 and T. Platt and T. Takagi (eds), *Punishment and Penal Discipline*, Crime and Social Justice Associates, Berkeley, California, 1979.

60. G. Hawkins, 'Prison labour and prison industries', *Crime and Justice: An Annual Review of Research*, 1983, 5. Robert Weiss, 'The reappearance of "the ideal factory"; the entrepreneur and social control in the contemporary prison', in J. Lowman, R. J. Menzies and T. S. Palys (eds), *Transcarceration: Essays in the Sociology of Social Control*, Gower, Aldershot, 1987.

61. B. Auerbach *et al.*, *A Guide to Effective Prison Industries*, vol. 1, *Creating Free Venture Prison Industries: Programme Considerations*, The American Foundation, Philadelphia, 1979.

62. *Op. cit.*, note 5, p. 55.
63. *Corrections Today*, June 1987, p. 113.
64. Francis T. Cullen, 'The privatization of treatment: prison reform in the 1990s', *Federal Probation*, March 1986.
65. J. J. McCarthy, 'Contracted medical care: prescription for change', *Corrections Magazine*, 3, 2, 1982, p. 9. Another subsidiary of a larger corporation operating in this service area is Correctional Care, a division of Emergency Medical Services Associates Inc.
66. *Ibid.*, p. 10.
67. *Ibid.*, pp. 14 and 16.
68. L. F. Norvick, 'The contractual model for medical care', *Medical Care*, 14, 8, 1976, p. 696.
69. *Op. cit.*, note 65, p. 9.
70. National Institute of Corrections, *Private Sector Involvement in Prison Services and Operations*, Washington, DC, 1984, p. 6.
71. *Corrections Today*, June 1987, p. 34.
72. P. B. Taft, 'The fiscal crisis in private corrections', *Corrections Magazine*, December 1982.
73. Report of the President's Commission on Privatization, *Privatization, Toward More Effective Government*, US Government, March 1988, p. 147.
74. P. Sweeney, 'Vision Quest's rites of passage', *Corrections Magazine*, 8, 1982, p. 24.
75. *Op. cit.*, note 73, p. 147. In 1975, 59 per cent of all juvenile detention and correctional institutions were operated by the private sector; by 1983 this had risen to 65 per cent.
76. P. Lerman, *Deinstitutionalization and the Welfare State*, Rutgers University Press, New Jersey, 1982, Chapter 7.
77. We are grateful to Pamela Swain in the United States Department of Justice for explaining just how the Bureau of Census compiled these figures.
78. *Op. cit.*, note 70, pp. 7 and 8.
79. F. Fox Piven and R. A. Cloward, *Poor People's Movements: Why they Succeed and How They Fail*, Pantheon Books, New York, 1977, Chapter 5.
80. For details of this expansion, the most significant in the USA since the 1930s, see R. M. Kramer, *Voluntary Agencies in the Welfare State*, University of California Press, Berkeley, 1981.
81. For some insights into the strategy adopted by the New Left at this time see W. Breines, *Community and Organization in the New Left 1962–1968. The Great Refusal*, Praeger, New York, 1982.
82. D. Altheide, 'Down to business: the commodification of non-profit social services', *Policy Studies Review*, 4, 6 May 1987.
83. While we use the concept somewhat differently, we are indebted to Altheide for the main thrust of this argument. For a more detailed and technical explanation of how human and welfare services came to be funded in the USA, so encouraging vendorism and the drift towards commodification, see *op. cit.*, note 80.
84. L. Curtis, 'The march of folly – crime and the underclass', in T. Hope and M. Shaw (eds), *Communities and Crime Reduction*, HMSO, London, 1987.
85. The National Council for Voluntary Organizations was interested enough to carry out a special study of the structure and operation of American welfare: see H. Lanning, *Government and Voluntary Sector in the USA*, NCVO, London, 1981.

86. 'Group aiding ex-convicts begins running of jail', *New York Times*, 17 February 1985.
87. The National Sheriffs' Association, *Position on Privatization of Adult Local Detention Facilities*, Alexandria, USA, pp. 1–3. The state of many American jails is reported to be deplorable. See, for example, J. Irwin, *The Jail: Managing the Underclass in American Society*, University of California Press, Berkeley, 1985.
88. *Ibid.*, p. 3.
89. Gerald W. McEntee, 'The case against privatization', *The Privatization Review*, Autumn 1985.
90. *Op. cit.*, note 31. Any attack on pensions would probably have federal support since Reagan's *Private Sector Survey of Cost Control*, looking at sources of 'waste and inefficiency' in federal government, found that the largest single source was state retirement pensions which were historically high to compensate for relatively lower wages. *Op. cit.*, C. H. Logan and S. A. Rausch, note 13.
91. *Op. cit.*, note 28, pp. 29–30.
92. *Ibid.*, pp. 33 and 36.
93. *Op. cit.*, notes 20 and 73.
94. *Op. cit.*, note 36.
95. *Op. cit.*, note 20, pp. 77–78.
96. *Op. cit.*, note 28, p. 25.
97. A copy of this resolution provided by Alvin Bronstein, American Civil Liberties Union, October 1987.
98. N. Wecht, 'Breaking the code of deference: judicial review of private prisons', *The Yale Law Journal*, 96, 787, 1987.
99. We think it impractical, but our prize for the most ingenious scheme to monitor the operation of private prisons, including disciplinary hearings, goes to J. T. Gentry who suggests the use of fines and bonuses. 'The panopticon revisited: the problem of monitoring private prisons', *Yale Law Journal*, 96, 353, 1986.
100. *Op. cit.*, note 20, p. 27.
101. *Ibid.*, p. 99. For some discussion of the complex legal background to this issue, see *op. cit.*, note 12, Mayer.
102. *Ibid.*, pp. 49–50.
103. Robbins, *op. cit.*, note 21. Notwithstanding this Concern the American Bar Association is currently preparing practical guidance on privatization in the form of a model contract and statute, see *op. cit.*, note 22, Robbins.
104. Provided by the American Correctional Association, June 1987.
105. *Op. cit.*, note 28, p. 16.
106. R. Immarigeon, 'Private prisons, private programs, and their implications for reducing reliance on imprisonment in the United States', *Pennsylvania Prison Society, The Prison Journal*, 65, 2, 1965.
107. *Ibid.*
108. R. Immarigeon, 'Prison bailout', *Dollars and Sense*, July/August 1987.
109. A. Hornblum, 'Are we ready for the privatization of American prisons?', *The Privatization Review*, Autumn 1985.
110. US Department of Justice, *Monday Morning Highlights*, 14 March 1988.
111. *Ibid.*

CHAPTER 3

Britain: interpreting the American experience

It is scarcely possible to conceive how a man, of Mr. Crawford's Christian principles, could have imbibed, with such an implicit faith, the overstrained estimate of good then predicated of the American Penitentiary system.[1]

So wrote one British prison governor of an influential official report of 1834. We shall come back to Mr. Crawford and his Christian principles in Chapter 4 when we examine some aspects of British penal history which bear on the current privatization debate, and the questions of principle which that debate raises. But we first want to examine the way in which the American experience of privatization has been imported into Britain, the latest in a long line of such imports since Crawford's day. 'New generation' prisons, the 'justice model', neighbourhood watch, reparation, 'policing by objectives', 'problem oriented policing' and now electronic 'tagging' – these are just some of the British state's more recent borrowings from American law enforcement. The process by which American ideas are imbibed varies from one case to another: sometimes the initiative comes from within the British state agency concerned;[2] in other instances, such as prison privatization, it is outside pressure groups and politicians who use the American experience as a precedent for change. But what all these examples have in common is that change is stimulated by events of which only a very small number of people in Britain have any detailed knowledge. The way in which that knowledge is mediated, through channels such as news reports, pressure group activity and the parliamentary process, is crucial in shaping the debate. The individuals and agencies involved, in our relatively small and centralized political system, are fewer in number and easier to identify than they might be in a comparable process in the United States.

PRESSURE GROUPS: THE ADAM SMITH INSTITUTE

It was the Adam Smith Institute (ASI), one of several right wing 'think tanks'

44

which have come to prominence under the present Conservative government, that first put the question of prison privatization on the political agenda. The ASI is in itself an interesting example of the two-way traffic in political ideas across the Atlantic. It was originally set up in Virginia in 1978 by two British intellectuals connected with the Heritage Foundation, the multi-million dollar pressure group of the American New Right. In 1981 the ASI was registered as a charity in Britain, with financial support from British United Industrialists.[3] Its former head of research, Peter Young, who did most of its work on private prisons, has also worked at the ASI's American office extolling the virtues of British free market policies to the American public.[4]

Just how much influence the ASI has is difficult to gauge as it works largely behind the scenes; but it boasts that many of its policies have been implemented by the Conservative government.[5] Many of these were promoted as part of the 'Omega Project' launched by the ASI in 1984,[6] and it was in the *Omega Report* on *Justice Policy* that the idea of private prisons made its British debut.

The Omega Project was an ambitious attempt to spell out the policy implications of the neo-liberal strand in New Right thinking and more specifically of the thought of Friedrich Hayek, then the chair of the ASI's academic board. Hayek has been characterized by Andrew Belsey as a 'conservative neo-liberal', whose emphasis on tradition (rather than natural rights) as the foundation of social order brings him close to the authoritarian conservatism of Roger Scruton.[7] On a theoretical level, however, the ASI's elaboration of Hayek's ideas is far removed from Scruton's reverence for the state. Not only does the *Omega Report* question the effectiveness of devoting more resources to law and order, it also asserts that 'The state's assumption of the main burden of responsibility in preventing, detecting and punishing crime may have helped generate additional crime by allowing individuals to escape (or forcing them to abandon) customary responsibilities that help keep crime down' (p. 20). But what at first looks like a radical attack on the law and order policies of the authoritarian Right ends up as a half-hearted endorsement of them: 'More policemen and stiffer sentences *may* have some effect on the crime rate, but cannot be expected to cure the problem by themselves'; 'There is a case' – we are not told what it is – for making 'life mean life, rather that "at least 20 years". Consideration of additional punishments, such as forced labour, *might* also be appropriate' [pp. 20, 55, our emphasis].

This is indeed reminiscent of Scruton's view that the appropriateness of 'flogging and maiming' offenders 'cannot be determined abstractly';[8] but its significance in the present context is that the sheer incoherence of the ASI's approach to the wider issues of penal policy helps explain the importance it attaches to privatization. It offers what the *Omega Report* otherwise signally fails to provide: a distinctively 'libertarian' solution to the problems of the penal system. Privatization, the report argues, can overcome both the spiralling costs of the prison system and the shortage of places, by using innovative managerial and technological methods and by concentrating resources on capital investment rather than increased labour costs (which the state system is said to favour because of the political pressure exerted by its workforce). As Peter Young has admitted,[9] when the ASI first proclaimed this message in 1984 not many people took it seriously. Things had changed by the time Young's own work on the American experience, *The Prison Cell*, was published by the ASI in 1987.

In 1984 the American private prison business was plainly at an embryonic stage, and the *Omega Report* does not conceal this fact. Yet only three years later, Young feels able to sum up his 'comprehensive review' of the American experience as follows.

> Whereas most comment to date has been theoretical speculation about what might result from prison privatization, such a review of the evidence can provide some hard conclusions based on the facts of what actually has happened.
>
> Perhaps the most surprising facts revealed by the report are the *greatly improved conditions for prisoners* in all the US private jails . . . That *costs can be cut* is not very surprising, given the general record of privatization, but that private firms can *both* cut costs and improve standards is certainly worth noting. Perhaps the most compelling argument for prison privatization is therefore the humanitarian one.
>
> (p. 38, Young's italics)

Young's 'hard conclusions' are, to put it politely, a shade premature. His claim that privatization cuts costs is, as we saw in Chapter 2, simply not borne out by the evidence. The crude cost comparisons he employs are of the type which Charles Logan, a leading US exponent of private prisons and author of one of the ASI's own publications on the subject (see below, Chapter 4), has described as 'almost useless'.[10] The 'general record of privatization' is not much clearer.[11]

What about the 'greatly improved conditions' in US private jails? Young's survey includes four case studies of jails (strictly speaking, three jails and a prison) which have passed from public to private management. One of these, in Santa Fe, New Mexico, had been run by the Corrections Corporation of America for only a few months and the favourable comments which Young quotes from local newspaper reports date from the transitional period before the hand over was completed. Of the remaining three we must place a question mark against one – Silverdale, the CCA establishment at Chattanooga – in view of the damaging evidence from the Prison Officers' Association which we shall look at later. That leaves two: Bay County Jail, Florida, which is a long way from our idea of a model prison (see p. 15), but is generally regarded as an improvement on the old regime; and Butler County Prison, Pennsylvania, on which we could find little independent information, apart from the fact that county officials claim that costs have *risen* under the new management.[12] There was evidently a great deal of room for improvement in both these institutions, and the ability of the private sector to run (at a loss, in CCA's case)[13] one or two show-places should come as no great surprise.

Despite the importance he attaches to the profit motive, Young's enthusiasm also extends to non-profit making American ventures. One of his most glowing descriptions is of Roseville, the women's jail run by Volunteers of America. By contrast, he devotes just thirty words to the Okeechobee School for Boys, the non-profit juvenile institution which we examined in Chapter 2, and makes no mention at all of the NIC's study of it, the one and only in-depth independent study of a private custodial institution, which found no evidence of improved conditions.[14] This is not the only major piece of evidence which Young overlooks. He refers to the National Institute of Justice only in connection with prison industries and of the reports by state governments he quotes only the one from Massachusetts which favours privatization.

Just as Young will hear no evil about the private sector he will see no good in anything done by government. His stereotype of the public sector as 'costly, insensitive and resistant to innovation' ignores the innovative record of the Federal Bureau of Prisons, particularly in pioneering 'new generation' prison design (the value of that particular innovation is another question). But perhaps the most startling examples of Young's selectivity are his statements that the 'day when the private sector starts to operate maximum security prisons is generally considered to be not far off' (p. 6) and that 'Most observers believe that prison privatization is set to expand in the US' (p. 37). The 'observers' quoted by Young turn out to be a CCA executive, a state congressman from Texas and the representatives of two firms involved in prison finance. With such a wide range of disinterested expertise to draw on, how can Young possibly be wrong?

Reading Young's eulogies on private prisons, we are reminded of some of the claims made in the nineteenth century for the new private lunatic asylums – institutions which very soon degenerated into custodial dumping grounds. As Andrew Scull says of the reforming mad–doctors, 'The ability to reduce the ambiguous to the certain, to order the world in an often grossly stereotypical fashion, is generally a necessary precondition if one is to be a successful moral crusader'[15] – and it is a quality that Peter Young possesses to a high degree. The full measure of his crusading zeal can be gauged from an article he wrote as Director of the US Adam Smith Institute, which urges supporters of free enterprise to set their sights on the privatization of the Soviet Post Office![16]

As we have said, it is not easy to assess just how much influence the ASI exerts behind the scenes. However, Michael Forsyth, the MP who according to the *Observer* played a leading role in promoting the idea of private prisons within the Conservative Party, has close links with the Institute.[17] By August 1986 the idea had been endorsed by a Conservative study group on crime,[18] and apparently attracted the attention of the Prime Minister herself. She it was, according to the *Sunday Telegraph*, who 'ordered' the visits to American private prisons by the junior Home Office minister, Lord Glenarthur, and by the Commons Select Committee on Home Affairs – a report Lord Glenarthur was quick to deny.[19]

THE HOME AFFAIRS COMMITTEE

The Select Committee on Home Affairs is one of several such committees which were introduced – after earlier abortive experiments – by the Thatcher government in 1980, largely as a means of strengthening parliamentary scrutiny of the executive. Since most backbench MPs (i.e. those who are not picked by the Prime Minister to serve in her governing team) generally have very little real input into the legislation passed by Parliament, membership of a select committee is one of the best chances they have, if they are government supporters, to influence their party leadership, or, if in opposition, to cause serious embarrassment to ministers or civil servants. The committees often play an important role in forcing issues and problems on to the political agenda. Typically, these problems will first have been brought to their attention by pressure groups, whose written and oral evidence makes a vital contribution to their proceedings. We shall see later how far this was true in the case of private prisons.

As the subject for its third report in the 1986/7 parliamentary session, the Home Affairs Committee chose to examine the state and use of prisons. As part of this investigation the committee exercised its power to travel abroad by visiting a number of prisons and non-custodial sentencing schemes in the United States. The issue of privatization was not specifically included in the Committee's remit, and according to Gerry Bermingham, one of the two Labour members who went on the American trip, it was only when they found that their timetable included visits to two establishments run by the Corrections Corporation of America (CCA) that they realized that the issue was on the agenda. How CCA came to have the necessary contacts to arrange this with the clerks who service the committee we do not know. The committee also visited two establishments for young offenders run by the Radio Corporation of America (RCA) at Cornwell Heights, Pennsylvania and Egg Harbor, New Jersey; we understand that these were included on the itinerary at the suggestion of the state governments concerned.[20] It was the work of CCA, however, which was to feature prominently in the committee's report.

How much were the members of the committee able to see of CCA's operations at Bay County Jail (together with its annex for juveniles) and the Shelby Training Centre, Memphis? It appears that they were able to talk quite freely to inmates and staff, though the inmates – according to David Clelland, the other Labour member of the party – were not very communicative. Gerry Bermingham thought that although their time was limited, a 'trained observer', and he included most MPs in this, could get 'a pretty shrewd idea' of how a prison was run, by asking 'the right questions – not necessarily of the obvious people'.[21] For example, by talking to the kitchen staff at Bay County he found that CCA appeared to have a good solution to the problems of serving hot food to prisoners, but he also formed the impression that 'the regime was not all that different' from what it had been under the old management; there were still problems of 'overcrowding and inadequate resources'. Both he and David Clelland accepted that Bay County was well designed, had been built in an impressively short time and appeared to be functioning smoothly. But they did not go nearly so far as the chair of the committee, Sir Edward Gardiner, who found CCA's operations 'stunning',[22] or the Conservative MP John Wheeler (Director-General of the British Security Industry Association and a former prison governor) who put out a press release declaring himself 'profoundly impressed'. During the committee's public hearings both Sir Edward and his Conservative colleague Jeremy Handley referred to their experience as something which had converted them from sceptics to enthusiasts for private prisons. As Jeremy Handley put it:

> It does seem that people are almost united in their revulsion of the idea of some private element within our prisons, if they have never seen them in operation. Similarly, the vast majority of people are united in their appreciation and understanding of what can be, and is, achieved by the so-called private prison systems, once they have actually seen them.[23]
>
> (Q221)

Yet this conversion was wrought, so far as we can tell, by a visit to just *one* privately managed adult jail, plus four juvenile institutions. There was no sign that the MPs had read any of the US research literature on privatization, although they had in fact been provided, by courtesy of the *British Journal of Criminology*, with copies of Shaheen Borna's useful article 'Free enterprise goes to prison'.[24] It was also somewhat misleading for Sir Edward to claim that when he and his colleagues 'asked the authorities whether they had found any fault in what we were looking at', they 'were faced with the reply that there had been no identification of any disadvantage' (Q4). According to Gerry Bermingham and David Clelland, the Tennessee authorities were far from being unanimously enthusiastic about private prisons and the state prison wardens they spoke to were vehemently opposed to the idea.

The committee returned to England deeply split over the privatization issue. Clelland and Bermingham strongly objected to the draft report on the American visit which the chair presented for the benefit of those members who had been unable to go. Clelland felt that it was quite inappropriate for one private company – CCA – to be 'mentioned about seven times' in the report, which in any case placed far too much emphasis on privatization, when the main purpose of the visit had ostensibly been to look at alternatives to custody. Both Clelland and Bermingham were opposed to privatization in principle, while one of the Conservative members, John Hunt, confessed to being less enthusiastic than his colleagues and advised the government to 'go very carefully indeed upon this matter' (Q35). Ivor Stanbrook, a Conservative member who was unable to take part in the visit, also remained unconvinced by the arguments for private prisons.[25]

It was John Wheeler who emerged as the most forceful advocate of 'contract management' in the committee's public hearings. He began by drawing a connection between privatization and another of the committee's main concerns:

the engine which has driven the authorities in the United States to contract out the management of their prison services has been the requirement of the courts, because there is a minimum standard of conditions of treatment for prisoners. Supposing there was a minimum standard laid down in English law, enforceable by the courts, would that not entirely transform many of the problems that we have had to put up with for decades in this country?

(Q10)

In other words, a code of minimum standards might force the Home Office to speed up the prison building programme to such an extent that it would be forced to turn to the private sector for help. It may well have been the possibility of making this kind of link between the causes usually advocated by penal reformers and a distinctively Conservative economic philosophy which appealed to Janet Fookes, an active member, like John Wheeler of the, Parliamentary All Party Penal Affairs Group and long regarded in the penal lobby as one of the most enlightened Tory MPs. She was quick to assure the Minister that she had 'no philosophical difficulties' about privatization and to ask him if he would be willing to meet members of CCA's staff 'on an informal basis' on one of their visits to England (Q14).

The committee's first witness was the Earl of Caithness, then Minister of State at the Home Office. He adopted a neutral position on the question of privatization, but did introduce one note of caution:

Although I am far less of an expert than any Member of the Committee who went to America, it does appear to me that the number of contracted-out or privatized prisons is relatively small in relation to the overall number of prisons . . . [T]he repercussions of doing something wrong would be far more noticeable in a small country like ours than spread out over the whole of the United States.

(Q35)

The Minister's rather exaggerated deference to the committee's superior knowledge reflected the painfully evident fact that he had not been well briefed on this subject. He acknowledged that 'No study has been carried out, nor any detailed thought given to the implications of the American experience in this respect for England and Wales' (Q1). Vivien Stern of the National Association for the Care and Resettlement of Offenders (NACRO) had interpreted this apparent apathy on the Home Office's part as a sign that privatization was unlikely to happen.[26] It certainly reflected a lack of enthusiasm on the part of many civil servants, but their failure to research the issue also made it easier for John Wheeler and his supporters to set themselves up as 'experts' on the American experience.

Of the three prison reform groups that gave evidence – NACRO, the Prison Reform Trust and the Howard League – only the Howard League submitted written evidence opposing privatization. The League had gathered a mass of American literature on the subject (which was initially of great assistance to us in writing this book) but the short paper which it submitted hardly did justice to the amount of research that went into it. However, it did show the 'embryonic' and 'marginal' extent of privatization in the United States to date, as well as succinctly formulating the main arguments of principle against private prisons; and it certainly did not deserve to be completely ignored, as it was in the committee's report. (To add a further insult, the League's evidence on the general question of imprisonment and penal policy was not even included in the published minutes.)

The Howard League also submitted a paper on 'Young people in custody' which, drawing on the American experience of the League's chairperson, Andrew Rutherford, praised the 'diversity and innovation' achieved in Massachusetts and Utah by contracting out the supervision of young offenders to non-profit making agencies.[27] As Rutherford stressed in his oral evidence (Q262) this is different from commercial privatization; but it is nevertheless difficult to reconcile with the League's insistence that the state must not 'abdicate responsibility' for the care of offenders.[28]

The only other organization which submitted detailed evidence on private prisons was the Prison Officers' Association (POA) which, like the committee, had arranged a trip to the USA to see private prisons at first hand. But as the union's chairperson, John Bartell, later commented, 'We and the Committee appear to have been on different continents.' Certainly they visited different prisons, the POA seeking out what Bartell called the 'flipside' of the corrections business, as opposed to the 'loss leaders' seen by the MPs. They also resorted to a degree of subterfuge; according to Bartell, the managements of the institutions they visited were under the impression that they were 'editors of penal reform magazines', and members of staff who were 'frightened to talk' were interviewed secretly, away from their workplaces.[29]

Of four establishments visited by the POA team, one, an unnamed juvenile institution, was described as 'well established and smooth running', though not particularly cheap; but their portrayal of the other three was damning.[30] At Hidden Valley Ranch, an institution for parole violators in Northern California, they were disturbed by the lack of privacy, the lack of staff on duty, the 'rows and rows of beds in a dirty dormitory', and the Warden's 'view that formal training was unnecessary and the best way for an officer to learn the job was to be "tossed in at the deep-end"'. But this was mild compared to their impressions of CCA's Houston Processing Centre for suspected illegal immigrants:

The inmates were contained in large dormitories each containing between 50 and 60 beds with no privacy whatsoever, no lockers, no screening around toilets or showers which were open to view by both male and female staff. Inmates . . . spent 23 hours per day in the dormitory. One officer supervised two of these units but did not normally enter the units. Inmates requiring any kind of assistance had to shout through the glass and metal doors. . . . The few officers we saw were scruffy and thug-like in appearance . . . [W]e have never witnessed such shocking conditions, which considering the state of some of our own prisons, is a terrible condemnation

51

in itself. We have never seen so many prisoners so obviously confused and despairing.

(para. 9)

Nor did CCA's Silverdale Penal Farm, Chattanooga, usually seen as something of a show-piece, emerge much better:

We saw evidence of inmates being cruelly treated, indeed the warden admitted that noisy and truculent prisoners are gagged with sticky-tape but this had caused a problem when an inmate almost choked to death. . . . Again showers and toilets were not screened and inmates, both male and female, were required to use these facilities in full view of other prisoners and staff. The level of supervision by staff was minimal. . . . The few staff we did see were clearly past what would be retiring age in any other system. . . . We were not impressed by [the warden's] frivolous and unprofessional attitude to his female charges. He continually made licentious remarks and described the impromptu 'strip-shows' which the inmates performed in the presence of male staff.

It is true that the POA team did not go to the United States with completely open minds and had an incentive to highlight the worst of what they saw; and there is certainly room for argument about whether what they describe is really any worse than many English local prisons or American county jails. But their observations undeniably cast doubt on the 'overstrained estimate of good' offered by the Conservative MPs and the Adam Smith Institute. The committee was also faced with the evidence of the prison governors' union (a branch of the Society of Civil and Public Servants) that their 'knowledge of the American privatization system would suggest that it can result in serious difficulties' (Q10) and that it was at best 'a curious irrelevance to the problems that the prison systems face in this country' (Q213). In fact, nowhere in the *Minutes of Evidence* is there a word of support for privatization from anyone except the Conservative MPs themselves.

The committee was able to reach a consensus on every issue except privatization and these agreed conclusions were published as its third report, *The State and Use of Prisons*. This included the recommendations that the prison building programme should continue; that crown immunity for prisons (immunity, that is, from health and safety legislation) should be phased out and a code of minimum standards introduced; and that the Home Office should study the use of electronic tagging in the USA.[31]

The privatization issue was discussed separately in the fourth report, which was supported by all the Conservative members who were present for the vote, while all the Labour members voted against it. Two Conservatives were absent: Ivor Stanbrook, who felt he did not know enough to form a considered view, and John Hunt. It was apparently at John Hunt's behest, however, that the report recommended private remand centres only 'as an experiment'.[32]

The fourth report runs to just under three pages. Its title, *Contract Provision of Prisons*, reflects its argument that it is 'not contemplating the "privatization"

of prisons', since privatization implies 'that the provider of a service is responsible only to his financial backers or shareholders and subject to market
competition', whereas prison contractors would be merely the 'agents' of a
public authority, subject to 'full inspection and the strictest supervision' (para.
2) – an argument which merely confirms David Donnison's observation that the
meaning of 'privatization' is 'at best uncertain and often tendentious'.[33] The
report begins by stating that 'During our visit to the USA we focused part of our
attention on prisons and youth custody institutions operated (and in some cases
built) by the Corrections Corporation of America.' The ambiguous phrasing
and repeated use of the plural neatly conceal the fact they only actually saw one
private prison. On this basis, the committee confidently asserts that 'contract
provision' of penal establishments:

1. relieves the tax payer of the immediate burden of having to pay for their
   initial capital cost;
2. dramatically accelerates their building; and
3. produces greatly enhanced architectural efficiency and excellence.

(para. 1)

The authors of the report apparently felt that their firsthand experience
entitled them to completely disregard the critical evidence of the Howard
League. But they cannot so easily dismiss the testimony of the POA, since they
too had seen private prisons at first hand. Since, moreover, they had visited
different private prisons from those seen by the committee, there is no basis for
questioning their veracity (though the description of their evidence as 'very
hostile' does suggest some suspicion of their motives). The committee is
therefore compelled to admit the possibility that its findings might not be
applicable to all private prisons, since its 'visits provided too small a sample upon
which to base general conclusions'. Abruptly changing tack, the committee
claims that its visits and the information supplied by CCA are merely 'an
illustration on the concept' of contract provision, the case for which:

rests fundamentally on two propositions, one theoretical and the other
practical. The practical proposition is the failure of the present state-
orientated system to overcome the problems of out of date and overcrowded prisons. The theoretical proposition is that the state should be the
sole provider of a service only when no-one else exists who can provide the
same service at less cost or can provide a better service.

(para. 9)

But what evidence is there, given the admitted limitations of the American
experience, that anyone exists who can do either? In a most peculiar move for a
group of Conservatives, the authors are reduced to placing the burden of proof
on the defenders of the *status quo*: 'There is no reason to suppose that privately
managed institutions could *not* improve conditions' (para. 14, emphasis added).
The committee could hardly have made a clearer admission of the bankruptcy of
its own argument.

In the delicately understated words of *Law Magazine*, the committee's report is 'not a distinguished contribution to penal literature',[34] and the most charitable view we can take of it is that it had to be rushed out in a hurry because it was known that a general election was in the offing and once it was called the committee would formally cease to exist. This was also one of the reasons the Labour members gave for their failure to produce a minority report. From our interviews with David Clelland and Gerry Bermingham we can surmise what the contents of such a report would have been: namely that punishment should be solely the business of the state; that private prisons created dangers of corruption (the most extreme example being that a wealthy criminal could – perhaps through a nominee company – actually buy out the prison where he or she was held); and that nothing could be achieved by privatization that could not be achieved by a properly resourced and managed state service. Interestingly, however, there was one form of private contracting of which both sides approved: the role of non-profit making agencies in providing juvenile facilities in Massachusetts.

Despite the poor quality of the committee's report, it undoubtedly achieved its object of pushing private prisons onto the political agenda. One measure of its success was the extensive media coverage which both the report and the committee's visit to America received.

THE ROLE OF THE MEDIA

Though all the print and broadcast media have played a part in importing the idea of private prisons from the United States, we want to concentrate, in the limited space available, primarily on the contribution of the newspapers and particularly those at the 'serious' end of the spectrum.[35] This seems justifiable as the private prisons debate is one where both sides have been more concerned with influencing policy makers (and especially MPs) than with reaching a mass audience, and it is the 'serious' dailies, and weeklies such as *The Economist*, which MPs look to as one of their main sources of information.[36]

The most striking feature of the press coverage of the American experience is that, although it is ostensibly 'foreign news', the immediate 'news event', the 'peg' which the story hangs on, is almost always drawn from British politics. Most news stories on the American experience are either reports of what, for example, the POA or the Adam Smith Institute has said about it or else are more detailed stories provided by way of background to the British debate (e.g. 'As Britain considers the privatization of prisons, Sarah Helm reports from the United States . . .').[37] In this the American coverage is quite different from that of the French government's proposals for private prisons, which received much less attention and, in the one paper that reported them in any depth (the *Financial Times*),[38] were treated solely as a matter of French domestic politics and particularly as a source of conflict between M. Chirac's government and President Mitterrand, who opposed privatization on principle. (One story in the *Guardian* (28 March 1987) did refer briefly to the French policy as one which might influence the Home Secretary – but the French government abandoned those particular proposals a few days later.)

One type of story which is conspicuous by its absence is that which treats its subject as one of the 'bizarre', 'larger than life' aspects of American society.[39] Private prisons are *not* depicted as 'the very latest and wackiest in penal servitude, the high technology, all-American, ultra-convenient method of paying your debt to society' – which is how the *Mail on Sunday* (7 September 1986) portrayed the first US experiments in electronic 'tagging'. The story on privatization which comes nearest to this tone (but with rather more wit and subtlety) is Aileen Ballantyne's 'How to buy the soft cell' in the *Guardian* (3 March 1987), which is about a scheme where offenders *pay* to be confined in a halfway house as an alternative to a prison sentence. Coupled with the fact that the only British group quoted as expressing interest in the scheme is the Adam Smith Institute, which most *Guardian* readers are likely to consider more than a little 'wacky', this sets it apart from 'normal' private prisons.

Far from treating such prisons as an oddity, press reports tend to ignore or play down those features of the American political system which, as we noted earlier, are most apt to appear odd to a British observer. A good example is another piece by Aileen Ballantyne describing how she accompanied the Home Affairs Committee MPs on their visits to two CCA establishments. Her report ends by suggesting that in both the USA and Britain, privatization provides an easy way of raising money for 'the essentially unpopular necessity of building new gaols', and therefore 'the attractions of the private sector are obvious'. But she does not mention the American system of funding capital spending through bond issues, which is a crucial factor in explaining the 'attraction of the private sector' and has no parallel in Britain. In fact, none of the ninety odd newspaper and magazine articles on private prisons we have traced mentions this issue. The three-tier system of prison administration is mentioned in a few articles, but in general, and not surprisingly given the need to establish the 'British interest' of the stories, the parallels between the two countries are given more prominence than the differences.

Apart from a few pieces of outright propaganda – including one in *Today* (27 August 1986) which even the Adam Smith Institute might consider over-zealous – the press is not open to anything like the same accusations of partisanship or distortion that can be levelled at the Home Affairs Committee or the ASI. There is ample coverage of the views of British and American critics of privatization (especially the POA), as well as supporters. Superficial changes like calling prisoners 'residents' get more attention than they deserve, but the *Sunday Times* (23 December 1984) tempers this with a dash of scepticism: 'The change of names does not disguise the fact that the tile and concrete cell blocks [at Silverdale] have the smell of a football club changing room and the charm of a public loo'. The reports in the *Daily Telegraph* (10 September 1986) and *Independent* (14 September 1986) also strike a sceptical note about the extent of privatization and the changes it has wrought. The *Observer* (4 October 1984) and the *Guardian* (28 October 1986), both papers with strong liberal repu-tations, carried relatively uncritical accounts. Overall, though, while none of the 'quality' papers dealt with the issue in outstanding depth, their coverage has been generally serious, unsensational and fair.

Of course, the decision that an idea is worthy of being treated seriously and fairly is itself a political judgement, as the *Guardian* recognized in an editorial (27 August 1986): 'The idea of "privatized prisons" is so inherently unlikely that it is difficult to take seriously . . . But don't mock it too much. The idea is up and running. Mrs Thatcher is tantalized by it.'

Well, if even the Prime Minister is interested, who could fail to take it seriously? But other papers were already treating the issue very seriously in 1984, when it was 'up and running' only on the far right of the Conservative Party. It is hard to imagine any left-wing Labour MP getting such favourable coverage for a radical new idea as Michael Forsyth received in the 'middle of the road' *Observer* (4 October 1984). Stories like that one – encouragingly headed 'Privatization: why not the prisons?' – and those in the *Telegraph* (21 May 1984) and the *Sunday Times* (23 December 1984) undoubtedly helped to put the idea on its feet.

Overt support came from the leader writers. While the *Guardian*'s editorial, after arguing that privatization should not be dismissed out of hand, finally came down against it, the *Sunday Times Business News* ('Memo to Maggie' 18 August 1985), *The Economist* (13 December 1986), *The Times* (8 May 1987), the *Telegraph* (15 May 1987) and the *Independent* (15 September 1987 and 26 July 1988) all unequivocally supported privatization, interpreting the American experience as showing how, in the *Independent*'s words, 'the market could . . . become the agent of reform in an area which desperately needs it'. *The Times* struck a strongly anti-union note, holding out its own battle with the print unions as an example the government should follow in tackling the POA. Both the *Telegraph* and *The Economist*, however, warned the government to proceed carefully to avoid causing public alarm. If the government follows the *Telegraph*'s advice and 'cautiously educates the public into the idea' of private prisons, then no doubt its supporters in what we anachronistically think of as Fleet Street will have an important part to play.

With the notable exception of a thoughtful *Panorama* report broadcast in 1985, television has so far devoted relatively little attention to the private prisons debate; but its future contribution could well be extremely significant. In a situation where eye witness evidence is at a premium, television pictures can make a powerful impact. Probably the most dramatic instance up to the time of writing (June 1988) is a short film on Silverdale broadcast on BBC television news on 6 May 1987, which appeared strikingly to confirm the POA's critical account of the same establishment:

Even in the maximum security wing, murderers, rapists and child molesters have only one overseer, who has to rely on new design and the very latest in security technology. Whole conversations with prisoners are made through the console. The officer mustn't leave his post.

The control of less violent inmates is also in the hands of a single officer, who is expected to keep his eyes on four separate units at once, each handling 32 men. Though most are sent out to work during the day, the rest of the time this place is their cell, their bathroom and their recreation hall. Privacy is out of the question even at the most intimate moments [Shot of naked man in shower].[40]

In a notable tribute to the power of the media, John Bartell of the POA – who had, in fact, seen private prisons for himself – told his annual conference a few days later, 'We have seen for ourselves the privatized part of the American penal system, because television has recorded the scenes of overcrowded dormitory accommodation, lack of privacy'.[41] In other words, Don't take my word for it, but the camera doesn't lie. For our part, we are more cautious about the weight to be attached either to a few minutes' video footage, or to accounts of brief visits by manifestly partisan observers; but it is by evidence of this kind, rather than by 'serious' research, that political and public opinion in Britain is likely to be moulded.

CONCLUSION

It always looked as if it would be difficult to sell the American experience of privatizing the penal system. The POA in particular was highly critical of the American experience, and while the Howard League was more measured, its early decision to oppose privatization on the basis of its own detailed research into what was happening in the USA was a signal which other lobby groups such as the Prison Reform Trust soon followed. The Labour Party also came out against the proposal, and the SLD was expected to join them.[42] Even among those Conservatives who took an interest in the issue there were differences, not only between members of the select committee, but between strong advocates of privatization like John Wheeler MP and a Home Secretary who began by being far from enthusiastic about this particular American import.[43] What evidence there is tends to suggest that Home Office civil servants supported the Home Secretary's stonewalling on this issue; and the announcement of a Green Paper on privatization in the remand system – a consultative rather than a policy document – seemed to confirm this view. True, the Home Secretary had moved to set up a new Prisons Building Board, which included private sector representatives, and private construction companies had been invited to submit proposals to it; but as the private sector already played a major role in prison design and construction and the new arrangements left the more contentious area of prison management untouched, this announcement was not seen as signalling any radical shift in official thinking.

This cool reception for their proposals did nothing to deter the pro-privatization lobby. John Wheeler continued to lobby behind the scenes, while Sir Edward Gardiner, who chaired the Home Affairs Committee when it studied the issue, has retired from parliament and now chairs Contract Prisons PLC, a new company part owned by the US corporation Pricor.[44] Pricor recently completed a new prison at Farmville, Virginia, and when the Home Affairs

Committee visited the USA again, this time to took at broadcasting, Pricor whisked them off in another executive jet for another guided tour.[45] The hard sell continued.

Such activities kept opponents of privatization on their guard; but nothing prepared them for the strong pro-privatization flavour of the Green Paper which was finally published in July 1988. Though formally presented as a discussion document, it leaves the reader in little doubt that the government is determined to go ahead and involve the private sector in the building and/or management of both new remand prisons and more secure bail hostels, as well as contracting out escort services for those awaiting trial.[46] The Home Office – and now, it seems, even the Home Secretary – has been persuaded that we should seriously consider yet another penal transplant from the USA. The third and fourth reports from the Home Affairs Committee are given generous praise for being 'constructive and informative' (para. 13). This is a remarkable claim for the fourth report which, apart from references to one company, the Corrections Corporation of America, is conspicuously *uninformative* about the American experience of privatization. Such generosity is probably best explained by the fact that the committee's willingness to use assertion in place of argument and evidence in discussing the American experience is surpassed only by the Green Paper itself. After a brief comparison of the British and American penal systems, and of the different political structures in which they each operate, the Green Paper goes on to claim that some of the important practical matters of principle which must be addressed in considering private sector involvement within Britain's prison system, such as maintaining standards, '*have* been overcome in the United States' (the Green Paper's emphasis, para. 23). No shred of evidence is offered in support of this assertion which, as we have already shown, many would contest. Nor are any references given; and yet it is on the basis of this intentionally comforting *assertion* that the Green Paper goes on to outline what privatization might look like in practice in Britain and what problems will need to be resolved – a clumsy sleight of hand if ever there was one.

However, it would be wrong to suggest that the debate in Britain has been conducted *wholly* on the basis of the American experience. On the contrary, Britain has its own experience of private involvement in the penal system to draw on, and in any case, the subject raises a number of issues important enough to have merited consideration in their own terms, with only limited reference to how they have been dealt with elsewhere. We shall discuss these precedents and issues in the next chapter.

NOTES

1. G. L. Chesterton, *Revelations of Prison Life*, Vol. 1, Garland, New York and London, 1985, p. 294.
2. For some examples, see M. Weatheritt, *Innovations in Policing*, Croom Helm, London, 1986.

3. D. Wade and J. Picardie, 'The Omega Project', *New Statesman*, 29 July 1983; 'Maintaining capitalism', *Labour Research*, 75, 2, 1985, pp. 45–8; P. Gordon and F. Klug, *New Right New Racism*, Searchlight, London, 1986, Appendix.

4. See, for example, P. Young, 'Follow Britain's lead on social security', *New York Times*, 26 January 1988.

5. J. Cunningham, 'The think tanks' role in the battle for Britain', the *Guardian*, 6 October 1987.

6. R. Levitas, 'Competition and compliance: the utopias of the new right', in R. Levitas (ed.), *The Ideology of the New Right*, Polity Press, Cambridge, 1986; Adam Smith Institute, *Justice Policy*, ASI Research, London, 1984.

7. A. Belsey, 'The New Right, social order and civil liberties', in R. Levitas, *The Ideology of the New Right*; R. Scruton, *The Meaning of Conservatism*, Penguin, Harmondsworth, 1980.

8. *Ibid.*, p. 84.

9. In the debate on 'Privatization and the prisons' organized by the Prison Reform Trust, London, 3 November 1987.

10. C. H. Logan, 'Proprietary prisons', in L. Goodstein and D. L. MacKenzie (eds), *The American Prison: Issues in Research and Policy*, Plenum, New York, forthcoming.

11. J. Kay, C. Mayer and D. Thompson, *Privatization and Regulation: The UK Experience*, Oxford University Press, Oxford, 1986. As K. Hartley and M. Huby's chapter 'Contracting-out policy: theory and evidence' in this volume shows, the contracting out of services can cut costs, largely by cutting the numbers, wages and fringe benefits of staff. Opponents of privatization argue that these staff cuts have led to a 'roughly proportionate' decrease in standards of service: see Labour Research Department, *Privatization: Paying the Price*, LRD, London, 1987, p. 11.

12. 'Warden defends Butler Prison', *Valley News Dispatch*, 15 April 1987.

13. 'Jail Inc. is popular but doesn't make a cent', the *Independent*, 1 August 1988.

14. See above, pp. 15–16.

15. A. Scull, *Museums of Madness*, Allen Lane, London, 1979, p. 98.

16. P. Young, 'Privatization around the world', *Proceedings of the Academy of Political Science*, 36, 3, 1987, pp. 191–205.

17. D. Hutchinson, 'Privatization: why not the prisons?', the *Observer*, 4 October 1984.

18. Conservative Study Group on Crime, *Prisons*, London, Conservative Study Group on Crime, 1986.

19. *Sunday Telegraph*, 24 August 1986; *Daily Telegraph*, 26 August 1986.

20. Interview with David Clelland MP, March 1988.

21. Interview with Gerry Bermingham MP, March 1988.

22. Quoted in the *Guardian*, 28 October 1986.

23. Question numbers refer to Home Affairs Committee, *State and Use of Prisons*, Vol. II: *Minutes of Evidence and Appendices*, 1986–87, HC 35-II, HMSO, London.

24. S. Borna, 'Free enterprise goes to prison', *British Journal of Criminology*, 26, 4, 1986, pp. 321–34; David Downes, personal communication.

25. Ivor Stanbrook MP, personal communication.

26. V. Stern, *Bricks of Shame*, Penguin, Harmondsworth, 1987, p. 159.

27. *Op. cit.*, note 23, p. 94.

28. Cf. M. Ryan and T. Ward, 'Privatization and the penal politics', in R. Matthews (ed.), *Privatizing Criminal Justice*, Sage, London, forthcoming.

29. All quotations are from John Bartell's speech in the 'Privatization and the prisons' debate (see note 9).

30. 'Memorandum submitted by the Prison Officers' Association', *op. cit.*, note 23, pp. 97–103.
31. For a commentary on the third report, see M. Ryan and T. Ward, 'Privatizing punishment', *Political Quarterly*, 59, 1, 1988, pp. 86–90.
32. Ivor Stanbrook MP and John Hunt MP, personal communications.
33. D. Donnison, 'The progressive potential of privatization', in J. LeGrand and R. Robinson (eds), *Privatization and the Welfare State*, Allen and Unwin, London, 1984.
34. 'Prisons for profit', *Law Magazine*, 15 May 1987.
35. We have traced around ninety British newspaper or magazine articles on private prisons from 1984 to June 1988, though this is very far from an exhaustive collection. Many of these are in the file compiled by the London Strategic Policy Unit and now held by the Police Research Unit, London Borough of Haringey. Others were located through a computer search carried out by the Thames Polytechnic Library.
36. J. Tunstall, *The Media in Britain*, Constable, London, 1983, p. 19.
37. The *Independent*, 14 September 1987.
38. The *Financial Times*, 28 October 1986, 20 November 1986, 9 April 1987.
39. S. Hall, C. Critcher, T. Jefferson, J. Clarke and B. Roberts, *Policing the Crisis: Mugging, the State and Law and Order*, Macmillan, London, 1978, p. 25.
40. Report by Bill Hamilton of the BBC, transcribed by the authors. *Channel 4 News* on the same evening carried a more detailed, but less sharply critical, feature on the two CCA establishments visited by the select committee.
41. Quoted in the *Independent*, 19 May 1987.
42. Robert McLennan MP, personal communication.
43. See for example *House of Commons Official Report*, 16 July 1987, col. 1299.
44. *NACRO News Digest*, May 1988.
45. Tony Worthington MP, personal communication.
46. The Green Paper was so positive that it was later described as 'a White Paper with a green border' by Nicholas Hopkins of UK Detention Services, a private consortium which includes McAlpine's, John Mowlem and the Corrections Corporation of America. (*File on 4*, BBC Radio 4, 14 November 1988.)

CHAPTER 4

Britain: precedents and issues

PRECEDENTS

The questions raised by the American experience of privatization are not altogether new to Britain. Private agencies have played a more substantial part in the evolution of the British penal system than is generally realized and before returning to the contemporary British debate we intend to explore this history further. There are four quite different precedents to be considered: the profit making prisons of the eighteenth century; the role of profit and private enterprise in the development of prison industry; the long tradition of private, mainly charitable, involvement in institutions for young offenders; and the running of immigration detention centres. (Private involvement in non-custodial sanctions will be left until Chapter 5.) These precedents are relevant to the current debate in at least two respects. First, they may not yield any clear cut 'lessons' about current issues, but like the American experience they can help us to see those issues more clearly and to identify some of the problems and arguments that may arise. We believe the history of private juvenile insti-tutions, which so far has been relatively neglected in the British debate, to be particularly pertinent in this respect. Second, history – often, again like the American experience, in a distorted form – has an influence on the current debate. In some ways, British penal history is very different from that of the USA – this is true especially of prison industry – and we would suggest that these differences have had significant effects on the two countries' political cultures.

Eighteenth-century prisons

The *Daily Telegraph* editorial on private prisons which we quoted in Chapter 3 was at pains to point out that 'We would not be talking about an avaricious

61

Hogarthian turnkey'. This is perfectly true. The avaricious turnkey portrayed by Hogarth (in *The Rake's Progress*, 1733–4) was not a contractor selling a service to the state, but a publicly appointed official who made most of his income by extracting fees from his prisoners. The natural consequence of this system of finance was that prisoners who had money (and owing to the intricacies of the eighteenth-century debt laws such prisoners were not uncommon)[1] could live in considerable comfort, while those who had none lived in the most dreadful squalor.[2] A further consequence was that prisons were not a major burden on the public purse and so the magistrates and sheriffs whose duty it was to oversee them had little leverage over the gaolers and little incentive to exercise what power they had. Whatever the defects in the accountability of modern private prisons, to equate them, as the prison historian J. E. Thomas did in the *Independent* (28 July 1987), with the prisons denounced by John Howard is surely to let rhetoric get the better of scholarship.

Nevertheless behind the rhetoric Thomas does have a valid historical point, which is that the idea that profit and punishment do not mix was established much earlier and more strongly in Britain than in the USA. Michael Ignatieff sees the turning point as the final rejection, in 1810, of Jeremy Bentham's offer to put his famous proposal for a 'Panopticon' into practice and run it himself as a private contractor. The parliamentary committee which considered Bentham's scheme accepted the view of the prison reformer G. O. Paul that it placed too much emphasis on the exploitation of convict labour, which ought always to be 'subservient to the great purpose of reformation through exclusion'. Ignatieff comments:

> In place of a Benthamite conception of authority regulated by market incentives, reformers like Paul succeeded in vindicating a bureaucratic formalism that looked to inspection and rules as the means to protect inmates against cruelty and to guarantee the rigour of punishment. For opponents of the contract system, punishment was too delicate a social function to be left to private entrepreneurs. For state power to preserve its legitimacy, it was essential that it remain untainted with the stain of commerce.[3]

Fee taking by gaolers was abolished five years later.[4]

Prison industry

The priority of reformation over commerce was reaffirmed in the 1834 report on American penitentiaries by William Crawford (whose 'Christian principles' and 'implicit faith' we met with in Chapter 3) and Whitworth Russell. What they advocated was not the Auburn system of silent associated labour, which in one form or another was adopted in the great majority of American prisons, but the rival Philadelphia system of unremitting solitary confinement. Though Crawford and Russell's 'Christian principles' played a part in this preference, an important underlying factor was pointed out by Beaumont and de Tocqueville, who undertook a similar mission to America on behalf of the French government: namely that prisons on the Auburn model could run at a profit in the unique economic conditions of the United States, but not in those of Europe (an insight later developed by Rusche and Kirchheimer in their Marxian analysis of the evolution of the prison).[5] As Melossi and Pavarini remark of the parallel debate in continental Europe:

> The marked lack of interest shown by European culture in the question of convict labour showed itself in the fact that the fundamental difference between the two systems – the one facilitating the installation of real productive work, the other not – was usually missed or at least was not seen for what it was.[6]

While the exploitation of convict labour played little part in the national penitentiary system, the picture was different in the prisons run by local government. Here productive industry was widespread and, in some instances, profitable. Some prisons made arrangements with private contractors, but rather than directly supervising the work, as was often the case in the United States, the contractors simply delivered the raw materials to the prison gates and took away the finished products. Even after the 1865 Prison Act, which severely restricted productive labour on the grounds that it was an insufficient deterrent, some local prisons contrived to make substantial profits.[7] The largest prison industries were mat making and oakum picking (oakum was made from old ropes and used for caulking wooden ships).

Although these industries continued after central government took control of the prisons in 1878, a rapid decline set in for several reasons. Under central government the prison rules were tightened up and the material incentives which had often been offered to both staff and prisoners to increase production were abolished. The oakum trade collapsed as wooden ships became obsolete. Centralization coincided, too, with a period of increasing agitation by organized labour, which was especially effective in destroying the prison matting industry. The number of prisoners engaged in mat making fell from 2,283 in 1876 to 186 in 1892/3 and their products were supplied only to government departments.[8]

The trades union representatives who gave evidence to the Gladstone Committee on prisons in 1895 were willing to accept the sale of prison-made goods provided that they were not sold below the market price and that 'every consideration [was] shown to the circumstances of particular industries outside to avoid all undue interference with the wages and employment of free labour'.[9] The Gladstone Committee agreed with these conditions. In practice, however, as the Departmental Committee on the Employment of Prisoners found in 1933, the English Prison Commissioners were 'deterred by the fear of objection from outside manufacturers or workpeople from undertaking any considerable volume of outside work'[10] and other government departments were virtually their only customers. Scottish prisons sold a larger proportion of their products on the outside market, but buying prison goods was the limit of private involvement. The 1933 Committee reaffirmed that the purpose of prison labour was neither punishment nor profit but 'the physical and moral regeneration of the prisoner', and it viewed the provision of additional work as a cost which had to be borne for that end, rather than a potential source of income. It also accepted that 'so far as possible prisoners should be employed in government work'.[11]

Thus the equivalent of a 'state-use' system was implemented, not by legislation as in the USA, but as a matter of government policy under pressure from employers and unions. It lasted until the 1970s when an attempt was made, in effect, to revive the nineteenth-century practice of producing goods under contract for outside firms. This programme was disastrously mismanaged, leading to heavy losses and to the trial and acquittal of several Prison Department officials on corruption charges.[12] After this fiasco the government decided that prison industries should once again seek their main markets within the prison service itself and among other government departments.[13]

Juvenile institutions

Among the early Victorian penal reformers who championed the idea of a system of juvenile reformatories, the issue of state versus private management was a contentious one. Some thought that such institutions should be a state responsibility, others that only private philanthropists could run them successfully.[14] The latter view rested on the belief that it was only through 'individual action on the human soul', as Mary Carpenter put it,[15] that juvenile delinquents could be reformed and only individuals who were motivated by religious benevolence were likely to achieve this effect. Carpenter and her supporters accepted, however, that the state had a role to play in two respects. First, since the new institutions would be subsidized from public funds, they would have to be inspected to ensure that those funds were properly used. Second, to the extent that they were *penal* institutions, concerned with upholding the criminal law, the state had a special interest in their management. In her proposals Carpenter drew a sharp distinction between industrial schools for children considered at risk of falling into crime, but convicted of nothing worse than vagrancy, and reformatory schools for those convicted of more serious offences:

> A penal line must then be drawn, and such schools must be far more distinctly under Government interference, and Government control, than any others; but I would carry individual action into these also.[16]

Carpenter's views, and the Government's reluctance to bear the entire cost of the new system,[17] prevailed. Reformatory schools were introduced by legislation in 1854 and industrial schools in 1857,[18] both under private management and initially – though this arrangement was short lived[19] – under two different systems of certification and inspection.

Whatever we think of the ideal of loving Christian discipline which inspired Carpenter, the reality of life in the schools was dismal. Tens of thousands of children were incarcerated for years, mostly for trivial offences, in conditions which were at best spartan, at worst horrifically brutal.[20] Chronic shortage of funds led the school managers to use industrial labour as a source of income rather than a means of training. In some schools the staff received bonus payments dependent on the amount of profit made. The inmates had good reason to feel that they were being 'used as mere instruments of gain',[21] especially when their release was delayed so that the school could hang on to their labour power.[22]

Problems like these, together with the low educational standards of the schools and the often dilatory conduct of the philanthropic managers, led a Home Office committee in 1896 to give serious thought to abolishing the system of private control, though it eventually came down against the idea.[23] A similar committee in 1913 saw the solution not in local government control, which by this time had been tried at a number of schools and found wanting, but in strengthening the woefully inadequate system of inspection;[24] and a Children's Branch of the Home Office was set up for this purpose. The new inspectors set about persuading the schools to abandon some of their more archaic features, which by this time were making them unpopular with the courts.[25]

The powers of the inspectorate were further strengthened in 1933, when the reformatory and industrial schools in England and Wales became approved schools. Almost every aspect of a school's regime had to be approved by the Chief Inspector: its dietary scale, daily routine, educational syllabus, system of rewards and privileges, even the children's pocket money.[26] Such close supervision was considered, in the words of the Ingleby Committee of 1959, to be 'necessary where the liberty of the subject is involved and where virtually the whole of the cost of the service is to be met from public funds'.[27] On paper, it looked as if the central state had assumed virtually complete control over the schools.[28] But the official inquiries into alleged abuses at particular schools in the post-war period revealed a different picture. The inspectors failed to prevent school managers, who needed to keep up the number of inmates in order for their school to earn sufficient fees to be viable, from exercising their powers over the release of inmates in flagrant disregard of the Approved School Rules,[29] or simply delegating them to the Headmaster.[30] At Standon Farm Approved School in 1947 the resentment of these practices among the inmates built up to the point where some of them murdered a master and absconded. A later scandal, which helped bring about the demise of the approved schools, stemmed from the conflict between conservative managers and the Home Office inspectorate over the use of corporal punishment.[31]

Contrary to the usual stereotypes of the state and of voluntary organizations, the voluntary managers acted, with rare exceptions,[32] as a consistently conservative force, and the Home Office as a relatively progressive one (the managers of schools run by local authorities seem to have been the most reactionary of all).[33] Though they played little part in the day to day running of the schools, the managers exerted a powerful influence over their general ethos, especially through the appointment of staff.[34]

In the years leading up to the replacement of approved schools by community homes with education (CHEs), the Home Office tried to persuade the schools to adopt 'therapeutic community' regimes.[35] But the inspectors it relied upon to achieve this end appear to have had almost exactly the opposite effect: their 'scrutinizing role inevitably increased the schools' preoccupation with organizational goals such as smooth running, purposeful activity and tranquility'.[36] The complicated bureaucratic structures within which the approved schools operated, the endless possibilities of conflict between the head, the staff, the managers, the inspectorate, the local authority and the national charities – themselves complex bureaucracies – which ran many schools (not to mention the children, whose views counted for very little), acted as strong disincentives to any action which might rock the boat.[37]

The CHEs which were phased in between 1969 and 1974 differ from approved schools in that children are not sentenced to be detained there by a court. The court places them in the care of a local authority (either because of an offence or for one of several other reasons) and the local authority may, at its discretion, place them in a home. Some CHEs and other children's homes are run by local authorities, some by voluntary organizations and others for profit.

There are no published figures on the number of profit making CHEs. In 1979 the Department of Health and Social Security estimated unofficially that there were 200 private (for profit) children's homes of various kinds,[38] but David Berridge, writing in 1983, could find only 71 and the number appeared to be shrinking.[39] A more recent survey by Martin Knapp, which does not claim to be exhaustive, covered 60 private children's homes, including 11 CHEs.[40] While a few entrepreneurs have made substantial profits from children's homes,[41] the typical home portrayed in Berridge's and Knapp's studies is a small family business, with modest profit margins, poorly paid staff and additional cheap, or free, labour contributed by the proprietor's family. Knapp suggests that the distinction between voluntary and for profit homes is often of little practical significance – local authorities are not always sure which is which and 'In many cases, the transformation of a private ("for-profit") home into a voluntary ("non-profit") home would be relatively straightforward and would likely result in no change of fees, operational policy or quality of provision'.[42]

From the point of view of the local authorities (mostly London boroughs) which use them, both types of private home offer good value for money, since they apparently provide as good a standard of care as those run by the councils themselves, and at significantly lower cost. But a hard pressed local authority can save more money by simply reducing its reliance on residential care and the fact that many authorities have taken this course[43] explains why (in contrast to care for the elderly and mentally ill) private child care has not enjoyed a boom under the Thatcher government.

Another contrast with care for the elderly and mentally ill is that private children's homes have been free from widespread allegations of serious abuses. The same cannot be said of two private facilities for 'disturbed' adolescents (most of them in local authority care and many with a history of offending) which featured in a BBC *Checkpoint* programme in 1984. St Andrews, Northampton was part of a non-profit private hospital, while Spyway, in Dorset, was a profit making 'nursing home'; but both shared the same medical consultants and both ran a regime of 'behaviour modification' in which food, clothing and liberty were regarded as 'privileges' to be 'earned'. They also employed a battery of powerful and potentially dangerous drugs.[44] After the programme was made, Spyway was taken over by the US hospital giant, American Medical International (see above, p. 25), who changed its name to the less Gothic-sounding Langton House, but made no fundamental changes in either its personnel or its regime.[45] (Langton House's controversial director, Gavin Tennent, has since left.) As *Checkpoint* pointed out, however, even worse abuses have occurred in the United States, where private adolescent units of this type are much more common, since private health insurance companies will often pay parents the cost of having their difficult teenage offspring locked up and 'treated'.[46]

Immigration detention

One of the more striking similarities between Britain and the USA is the use which both countries make of the private sector's services in detaining suspected illegal immigrants. Although the detention centres serving Heathrow and Gatwick airports are ultimately the responsibility of the Home Office's Immigration and Nationality Department, both the provision of security staff and the transportation of detainees to and from the centres are contracted out to a private security firm. Securicor was awarded the contract (by a Labour government) in 1970, when the Home Office took over from the airlines the responsibility for detaining people refused entry to Britain, and they retained it until just before this book went to press, when their leading rival, Group 4 Total Security Ltd, put in a lower bid and won the contract from them.[47] It appears that Securicor was given the original contract on the grounds that it would be cheaper than employing prison officers.[48] However, in March 1987 the government revealed that it cost £115 a day to detain a person in an immigration service detention centre (including transport, escort and running costs), but only £34 a day to detain an immigration prisoner in a prison department establishment.[49] It would be misleading to treat these two figures as directly comparable, but given the pro-privatization lobby's fondness for equally misleading cost comparisons, they can hardly complain if their opponents seize upon this one.

In the year ending 2 April 1988, 12,802 people were detained in the immigration service detention centres staffed by Securicor. This includes 198 on board the ferry *Earl William*, leased by the Home Office from the privatized shipping company Sealink – the only British example so far of a prison leasing agreement – and used as a detention centre from May 1988 until it came adrift in the severe storm of 16 October.[50] Although most were detained for no more than a day or two, some of those in Harmondsworth, the main centre serving Heathrow Airport, and on board the *Earl William*, spent weeks or months in custody. On the *Earl William*, which was used mainly for entrants claiming refugee status, inmates complained that the ship was not equipped to deal with long term residents (women detainees were not even provided with sanitary towels).[51] Two Tamils who had fled from Sri Lanka went on hunger strike; two others jumped ship.[52]

The Government's Green Paper on *Private Sector Involvement in the Remand System* refers to the experience of airport detention as an important precedent for the contracting-out of custodial duties (para. 47), but Stephen Shaw of the Prison Reform Trust has suggested that the precedent is in some ways a worrying one.[53] He points to the lack of staff training – seven days on the general work of Securicor and just one day on their duties at the centre[54] – and their lack of accountability. Although each centre is inspected daily by a Home Office official of at least the rank of Chief Immigration Officer, there is no Board of Visitors (the panel of lay people which serves as a 'watchdog' in Prison Department establishments) and the questions which can be asked in Parliament are restricted by considerations of 'commercial confidence'.[55] There have also been some complaints of detainees being bullied by staff.[56] When Shaw's article was published in the quarterly bulletin of the Association of Members of Boards of Visitors, the editor added a note about a colleague who had been detained at Harmondsworth, and 'found the Securicor staff very racist and unkind to detainees'.

It would be wrong to suggest that the particular weaknesses in the accountability of immigration detention centres, or the particular abuses which occurred in privately run reformatories and approved schools, would *necessarily* be reproduced in British private prisons. These examples do serve, however, to reinforce the impression we have gained from the American experience that the accountability of private institutions, and the potential for abuse of their discretionary powers, pose severe problems. Particularly noteworthy in this respect is the way in which the state's efforts to strengthen the accountability of private juvenile institutions not only failed to prevent abuses but reinforced a conservative and unimaginative style of management which was just the opposite of what privatization is supposed to achieve.

On the other hand, the long history of privately run penal institutions in Britain sets in perspective some of the allegedly fundamental objections to privatization which we shall examine in a moment. In looking at these objections, it is noticeable that the opposition to private prisons in Britain has tended be couched in rather more fundamental terms than in the USA. Greater reliance seems to be placed here on the view that it is simply wrong for the state to renounce any part of its responsibility for prisoners' welfare, or alternatively (and these two propositions are not always clearly distinguished) that it is wrong to make punishment a source of private gain. Such arguments are by no means unknown in the USA, but we would suggest that they have a greater resonance in Britain's political culture and that this is partly a legacy of the divergent penal histories of the two countries. It is with these arguments that we begin our consideration of the issues of principle raised by the private prisons debate.

ISSUES

Delegating the power to punish

Apart from penal history, another feature of British political culture which contributes to the opposition to private prisons is monarchism.[57] Douglas Hurd, for example, has declared that 'The business of keeping convicted prisoners in Her Majesty's prisons – because Her Majesty's courts have so decreed: that is the business of Government.'[58] The Howard League likewise argues that 'People are imprisoned in the name of the Sovereign and this cannot be delegated to someone else.'[59] (It is hard to imagine anyone talking in quite this way about, say, Bay County, Florida.) Andrew Rutherford of the Howard League put the same point in more democratic language when he addressed the Parliamentary All-Party Penal Affairs Group on the case against private prisons:

> Prisons were a public trust to be administered on behalf of the community in the name of justice. To open the way for the private sector into the administration of prisons would undermine the very essence of a liberal democratic state.[60]

Opponents of privatization use a lot of this kind of rhetoric, but they never seem able to say with any precision *why* the private administration of prisons would threaten the 'essence' of the state. It is important to remind ourselves here that we are not discussing the legislative and judicial *allocation* of punishment, but only its *delivery*. As we have seen, there is nothing very new (or very archaic) about entrusting the delivery of punishment to private agencies, and Rutherford himself supports the contracting out of some (fairly intrusive) forms of non-custodial supervision.[61] So what is special about prisons?

The most plausible answer to this question, in our view, is that prisons rely *directly* upon the organized use of force. Non-custodial supervision is backed by the threat of force but (at least in the British system) force is rarely used in the actual administration of the sentence. Reformatories and approved schools did rely on the direct use of force to a certain extent, but this could be legitimated by an analogy with other private agencies, i.e. parents and non-penal schools. The degree of coercion required to run a prison, on the other hand, is far more substantial and would amount to a significant delegation of that 'monopoly of the legitimate use of force' which Weber defined as a fundamental characteristic of the modern state.[62]

The term 'monopoly', however, with its connotations of ownership, is a somewhat misleading one in this context. The 'monopoly' claimed by the state – primarily in its legislative and judicial aspects – is over the power to *define* the legitimate use of force within its territory, and this power does not necessarily depend on the state (the executive) *owning* the means of force or *employing* the individuals who use it. As Charles Logan puts it in a paper published in England by the Adam Smith Institute:

In a system characterized by rule of law, state agencies and private agencies alike are bound by the law. For actors within either type of agency it is the law, not the civil status of the actor, that determines whether any particular use of force is legitimate. The law may specify that those authorized to use force in particular situations should be licensed or deputized and adequately trained for this purpose, but they need not be state employees.[63]

While this is correct in principle, we should point out that in reality the organized use of force in liberal democratic states only very imperfectly approximates to the 'rule of law'.[64] The potential for abuse is a strong reason for proceeding with caution before entrusting to *any* agency, public or private, powers to use force which it has not previously possessed. It is not, by itself, sufficient to render privatization absolutely inadmissible, but it is a ground for insisting that only fairly weighty reasons could justify the risks which privatization entails.

Profit and ethics

Many people, ourselves included, feel that it is morally repugnant to punish people – that is, to engage in the deliberate infliction of suffering – for the sake of profit, in much the same way that is repugnant for mercenaries to kill people for profit. What is unjust about private prisons, according to this view, is not (or not only) the punishment inflicted on the inmates, but the rewards that accrue to penal entrepreneurs. The advocates of privatization would retort that most of the people who work in the state penal system are paid for their labour, and 'that is just another profit motive'.[65] This argument ignores the distinction between those who sell their labour power (and may have very limited choice about whom they sell it to) and those who own and control capital; and it also ignores the fact that many of those who engage in the distasteful business of inflicting pain do so not simply for economic reasons, but in the hope of mitigating the full impact of what they see as a regrettable social necessity. To equate their contribution with that of corporate executives and shareholders who are simply out to make a 'fast buck' seems to us to be highly misleading. Equally misleading is Young's analogy with grocers, who 'make a profit by catering for human hunger';[66] a better analogy would be with people who make a profit by deliberately starving others.

But the moral case against privatization is also bound up with the moral argument against the present excessive level of punishment. We agree with Nils Christie that the overriding moral imperative in the field of punishment is to reduce the level of pain infliction as far as possible. It is compatible with that goal to pay those whose job it is to inflict pain a reasonable wage, but not to create arrangements by which people get rich in direct proportion to the quantum of pain they inflict.[67]

Political pressures

To put what is essentially the same point in political rather than moral terms, there are clear dangers in creating a 'penal–industrial complex' with a vested interest in an expansionist penal policy.[68] One of many critics who have made this point is the Labour MP Brian Sedgemore:

> It would be in the interests of prison entrepreneurs to support longer sentences and have more people put in prison. That would be a disaster of the highest magnitude as sentencing policy is already excessive in this country.[69]

This is also one of the main anxieties that has been expressed in the American debate[70] and we do not regard it by any means as a fanciful suggestion. The companies which have already expressed an interest in private prisons include McAlpine and John Mowlem, both wealthy and powerful corporations and both substantial contributors to Conservative Party funds.[71] A meeting to discuss prison privatization at the Carlton Club in 1988 shows just how closely political and business interests are beginning to work on this issue. The meeting in question was attended by over 100 people, including representatives from the City, security firms and the building industry, addressed and chaired by the former chairperson of the Commons Home Affairs Committee, who now chairs Contract Prisons PLC.[72]

Ironically, the Adam Smith Institute, itself a pressure group funded by commercial interests, has argued for privatization as a means of freeing the prison system from the political pressures created by fears of strikes, unemployment and the electoral unpopularity of penal reform.[73] There are certainly enough political pressures which militate against penal reform without risking the creation of another one.

Prison discipline

One of the main problems to emerge both from the American experience of private prisons and the British experience of private juvenile institutions is the danger that such institutions may abuse their disciplinary powers and particularly their power to determine or influence an inmate's date of release. If this were merely a matter of conducting formal disciplinary hearings it might be possible to solve the problem by insisting that all such hearings be conducted by independent, state appointed officials; although some advocates of privatization, such as Logan, as well as opponents such as the POA, are unhappy with such proposals, which they see as undermining management's control of the institution.[74] It could alternatively be argued that since even a state appointed prison governor cannot seriously claim to be an independent and impartial judge in disputes between prisoners and staff, the fact that he or she might have an indirect pecuniary interest in a prisoner's loss of remission is of relatively little consequence.

In many ways, however, the role of prison staff is more closely analagous to that of the police than to that of the judiciary (indeed a prison officer enjoys 'all the powers, authority, protection and privileges of a constable').[75] Like the police, they have extensive discretionary power and the exercise of this discretion is not merely a series of isolated decisions, but can reflect a systematic policy or characteristic style, with profound effects on the lives of those subjected to it. Women prisoners, for example, often experience minutely detailed regulation based on the staff's notions of 'womanly propriety'.[76] It is difficult to see how an institution's style of rule enforcement could be effectively supervised but quite easy to imagine how it could be affected by a contractor's vested interests.

Alongside the formal disciplinary system, moreover, there exists an 'informal' or 'shadow' system whose sanctions include segregation 'in the interests of good order and discipline', withdrawal of privileges, transfers to other prisons, etc. If managers and staff find the formal system not to their liking, they may turn to these measures instead.[77] Finally, it is not unknown for prison officers to resort to illegal violence as a means of punishment and control.[78] If every possible check were employed against abuse of lawful methods – by severely restricting and monitoring the use of informal sanctions and paying the contractor nothing for detaining prisoners beyond their earliest dates of release – this could lead to acts of brutality by frustrated officers. In short, while it is difficult if not impossible to subject the disciplinary methods of any prison to thorough external control, in the case of private prisons the possibility of vested interests, and the conflict between outside supervision and the independence of a private body, pose additional problems.

Effects on the system

John Lea, Roger Matthews and Jock Young have argued, on the basis of research on the US juvenile justice system, that privatization would lead to 'the construction of a two-tier system of punishment', with private institutions creaming off the less serious and more tractable offenders.[79] The dangers inherent in this process are, first, that the prisoners who are left in the public sector are defined as a 'hard core' for whom nothing can be done; and secondly that the private sector is able to make spurious claims to greater efficiency and humanity. As we noted in Chapter 2, there may also be a differential impact on women prisoners. Their relatively small absolute numbers and predominantly low security risk mean that a small number of private establishments could have a proportionately much greater impact on them than on the male prison population, making the danger of a 'two-tier' system especially acute. The fact that a large proportion of women prisoners are on remand is also significant in view of the government's Green Paper.

The Green Paper, while arguing that in principle the private sector could be entrusted with all but very high risk (Category A) remand prisoners, acknowledges that private institutions might be willing or able to accept only low security inmates (para. 86), and it might be necessary to establish a new system for classifying remand prisoners by security risk. At present, remand prisoners are treated as either being 'potentially category A status', or 'unclassified', which in practice means that they are held in conditions appropriate to the second highest level of security risk, category B. As the Green Paper points out:

> Only about 50% of remand prisoners are given custodial sentences, and some 50% of those are eventually categorized C or D. This suggests that a large number of remand prisoners may be held in higher security establishments than is necessary. It is possible, therefore, that the introduction of private sector remand establishments suitable only for lower security inmates would contribute to cost-effectiveness by . . . securing a better match between the prisoner and the security of the establishment . . .
>
> (para. 871)

Any such savings would have nothing whatever to do with whether the low security establishments were private or public, but could be a useful source of misleading cost comparisons for the privatization lobby.

Max Taylor and Ken Pease, two of the more sophisticated advocates of privatization, see the possibility of such spurious claims to greater efficiency as one of the main dangers their proposals must avoid.[80] They suggest the ingenious but unrealistic solution that private contracting should initially be restricted to sentenced prisoners serving 18 months or more. Even before the Green Paper was published, it should have been obvious (particularly to two writers who set great store by their political realism) that no government, and no contractor, was likely to run the risks inherent in conducting an *experiment* in privatization at the deep end of the system.

Two more advocates of privatization, Roger Hall and Neville Woodhead, have argued that it would achieve genuine savings because making each prison a separate economic unit would promote better financial management.[81] They argue that while in theory it would be possible to introduce a more decentralized and efficient managerial system without resorting to privatization, the Home Office's record is such as to make this unlikely. The ham fisted application to the prisons of the government's financial management initiative,[82] which was supposed to achieve much the same thing,[83] would appear to lend some weight to this argument. But even if a few prisons are privatized, the state will have to go on managing the greater part of the system for the foreseeable future and this role cannot simply be given up as a bad job. Privatization *might* lead to more efficient financial management in a few prisons; but to treat this as being a central objective of penal policy in our view places far too high a value on efficiency.

Effects on regimes

Some advocates of privatization do not rest their case on efficiency alone, but claim that privatization would lead to more humane, or even rehabilitative, regimes. The simplest version of the argument, advanced by Logan and the ASI, is that the profit motive is a powerful incentive to treat prisoners well:

> The exercise of naked power is extremely costly; co-operation is much more cost-effective (and therefore profitable) than coercion. Commercial prisons, unlike the state, cannot indefinitely absorb or pass along to taxpayers the cost of riots, high insurance rates, extensive litigation by maltreated prisoners, cancellations of poorly performed or controversial contracts, or even just too much adverse publicity.[84]

If the benefits of humane treatment are so evident, it is not clear why they should not provide a sufficient incentive in institutions governed by the 'convenience motive' which according to Logan characterizes state bureaucracies. After all, riots, lawsuits and bad publicity are all considerable inconveniences. This is too complex a question to be resolved by Logan's rather simplistic political analysis, but a part of the answer is that, in many British prisons, it has – at least until recently – been possible to warehouse remand and short-term prisoners in the most revolting conditions *without* creating any major problems of control. Inhumanity is not necessarily either costly or inconvenient. Nevertheless, there is a measure of truth in Logan's argument. Precisely because the legitimacy of private prisons would, in the early days at least, be open to question, they could well be more vulnerable to adverse publicity, and to protests by prisoners, than the state system is. In the short term, then, privatization could offer some tactical advantages to prisoners and penal reformers; but these would tend to diminish once the novelty of private prisons wore off.

Taylor and Pease advance an even bolder case than Logan's, claiming that it would be possible to introduce an 'incentive to rehabilitate' by making part of the contractor's fee dependent on a prisoner avoiding reconviction for a certain time after release. This argument obviously depends on the belief that, contrary to present conventional wisdom, prison regimes can have significant rehabilitative effects (so, incidentally, does Lea *et al.*'s argument that private contractors would have an incentive *not* to rehabilitate). Given the crucial importance of this point, it is unfortunate that Taylor and Pease give no details at all of the 'possible techniques for change' which they claim have been identified in (unspecified) research literature but never tried in prisons.[85] Others would argue that, even if the view that 'nothing works' is too simple, prison is an inherently unsuitable environment for individual treatment.[86] There must, at the very least, be a strong possibility that measures aimed at earning a 'no reconviction bonus' would fail, and the contractor would then have to make cuts in the regime to avoid losing money. There would be no incentive, under Taylor and Pease's scheme, to spend money on purely humanitarian measures which simply make prison life more bearable; they are emphatic that reconviction measures should be the sole test of success.

The most likely effect of privatization on prison regimes is, we would suggest, that private companies will tend to minimize their labour costs and rely on more' capital-intensive forms of control. This is, in fact, one of the main advantages that Young and the ASI see in privatization and it seems to have been realized to some extent in CCA establishments like Silverdale. A high staff/inmate ratio is certainly not a sufficient condition for a humane regime – it can be thoroughly oppressive – but it does appear to be a necessary one. For example, the Dutch prison system, which perhaps comes as close as any to relying on cooperation rather than 'naked power', has twice as many personnel per 100 prisoners as England.[87]

Accountability

At first sight the issue of accountability is one where the advocates of privatization appear to have a strong case. The great merit of privatization, it is argued, is that it separates out the day to day administration of prisons from the Home Office's responsibilities for supervising them and upholding standards. At present the Home Office not only runs prisons, it also appoints the lay Boards of Visitors which act both as watchdogs and disciplinary tribunals, while the Inspectorate of Prisons forms part of the Home Office and is mainly staffed by seconded prison governors. Privatization would at least go some way towards breaking this monopoly. As the *Independent* (26 July 1988) put it in an editorial on the government's Green Paper:

> it is not in human nature to impose the most exacting standards on oneself. It is much more likely that the Home Office will develop into the tough regulatory body needed by British prisons if it is not also running them.

However, similar common sense objections about 'human nature' can be made to the Green Paper's proposals, by which a 'a monitor (a Home Office official) might either be stationed in, or regularly visit, a contracted-out remand centre, and report on its performance to the Home Secretary through the Prison Department' (para. 65). The difficulty with this kind of arrangement is summed up by Vagg, Morgan and Maguire in their book *Accountability and Prisons*: 'regulatory bodies . . . may find themselves co-opted into the values and goals of the bodies they are required to regulate, thus losing the critical eye of the outside oberver'.[88] This danger would be particularly acute for a body so heavily reliant on a single official who would spend much of his/her working life inside the institution s/he was required to monitor.

The Green Paper is disconcertingly vague on other crucial questions relating to accountability, stating for example that:

> Consideration will need to be given to whether privately-managed remand institutions should be subject to inspection by HM Inspectorate of Prisons, and whether they should have Boards of Visitors, like other establishments.
>
> (para. 67)

Although the Green Paper recognizes the need for 'clear and enforceable standards' (para. 69), these would be purely contractual requirements, enforceable only by the Home Office itself, not statutory minimum standards which

75

prisoners could enforce through the courts (in the USA, where different legal principles apply, a prisoner probably *can* sue for breach of a contractual standard).[88] The issue of 'commercial confidentiality' of information receives only a passing mention as something about which 'decisions will have to be taken' (para. 66). It is briefly acknowledged that 'suitable means of redress' must be provided for prisoners who consider themselves mistreated, but there is no discussion of whether this would be against the contractor, the government or both (para. 92). Though it appears self-evident that private prisons would not enjoy crown immunity, the implications of this are not mentioned. And, although the Green Paper appears to assume the privatization will require new legislation, there is no discussion of whether privatization is compatible with the Prisons Act 1952, in particular section 4(1): 'The Secretary of State shall have the general superintendence of prisons and shall make the contracts and do the acts necessary for the maintenance of prisons and the maintenance of prisoners.'[90]

It is not the function of a Green Paper to set out every detail of the arrangements it contemplates and in this case it is made clear that management consultants have been engaged to work on the finer points; but what is worrying is that the government appears to think that the proposed monitoring arrangements alone may be sufficient to meet concerns about the accountability of private remand centres. As we noted earlier, this confidence is based on the spurious notion that the effectiveness of such arrangements has already been proved in the USA. The government's current proposals are clearly vulnerable to attack on this front.

Some opponents of privatization weaken their case, however, by their readiness to take at face value the prevailing constitutional fictions about the accountability of *public* prisons. J. E. Thomas, for example, passionately affirms that 'we cannot sweep aside the compelling legal and moral reasons for holding on to our responsibility and accountability for our prisoners'.[91] But what does this 'responsibility and accountability' really amount to? The fact is that 'our' elected representatives play only a very limited role in formulating penal *policy*[92] – a role which they would still play after privatization – and their (let alone 'our') responsibility for what happens in individual prisons is negligible. Admittedly the Home Secretary is accountable to Parliament in the narrow and literal sense that s/he can be required to give an account of what happens in prisons, and it will be important to ensure that if prisons are privatized the Home Office, as the ministry responsible for maintaining standards, is required to make the same kinds of information available ('commercial confidentiality' notwithstanding). But if all the penal lobby is concerned with is preserving the existing forms of accountability, it is far from clear why this should lead it to oppose privatization root and branch.

What is missing, not only from the privatization debate but from the debate about prisons generally, is any adequate model of what genuine democratic accountability applied to prisons would look like. The unique characteristics of prisons make this a very complex question which we cannot discuss adequately here. Among the issues which need to be explored are: the prospects for developing a degree of internal democracy, involving prisoners and prison officers (the example of the Barlinnie Special Unit in Scotland is important here);[93] the formulation and enforcement of minimum standards; the integration of prison medicine and education into the outside system of educational and medical administration;[94] the role of local authorities (the Left has sadly failed to extend the police accountability debate to prisons); and the reform of Boards of Visitors, stripping them of their disciplinary functions and perhaps placing them under the auspices of local rather than central government. Related to this is the issue of legal accountability: the creation of a range of legally enforceable rights for prisoners.[95]

There is, in theory, no reason why any of these forms of accountability should not apply to private institutions as well as to public ones. As Roger Matthews points out, the difference between a public and a private body may be of minimal significance if both have identical forms of accountability.[96] What this argument overlooks, however, is that is precisely the *lack* of public accountability in the private sector – viewed as freedom from 'red tape' and political pressures – which is alleged to enable it both to save money and to pursue new managerial solutions to the prison crisis.[97] The Green Paper recognizes this, arguing that 'In order to give scope for innovative solutions to problems, it will be important for standards to be defined so far as possible in terms of the results to be achieved, rather than the means to be employed' (para. 12). Yet the 'means' may be no less important than the 'ends' from the point of view of the prisoners' quality of life, particularly if the means are of the high technology, labour saving type which we have suggested is likely. The task facing the Left and the penal lobby is to think through how decisions on such matters can be democratized; to devise procedures which allow both prisoners and ordinary citizens to make a real input, while recognizing the requirements of security and expert knowledge. Difficult as this is, it clearly entails something very different from leaving things to the discretion of managers whose paramount duty is to their company's shareholders.

Remand prisoners

In limiting its proposals, initially at least, to the remand system, the government is following the view taken by nearly all the British advocates of privatization, with the exception of Taylor and Pease. The Green Paper points to the severe pressures on the existing institutions where remand prisoners are held (para. 2). It also points out that the questions raised above about the involvement of private organizations in prison discipline

> either do not arise, or at least are less significant, in dealing with remand prisoners . . . [since] time spent on remand is reliant on decisions of the courts in which the prison authorities have no role. But remand prisoners can lose prospective remission and decisions would have to be taken about whether this sanction should be retained in private facilities and, if so, how it should be exercised.
>
> (para. 29)

To allow private contractors themselves to exercise this power would be, in effect, to place part of the state's own penal resources at their disposal: an anomalous position, to say the least.

However, the fundamental objection to the private provision of additional remand facilities is that, in seeking to speed up the provision of new accommodation, it is tackling the problem from the wrong end. Scandalous as conditions for remand prisoners are, the greater scandal is the excessive number of people remanded in custody despite the 'presumption of bail' supposedly enshrined in the Bail Act, 1976.[98] The Green Paper does recognize the need to increase the granting of bail and the Home Secretary has criticized the magistrates' over-use of remand;[99] but the government's attitude still falls far short of the recognition which might be expected from a liberal state, that the incarceration of a presumptively innocent person is such a grievous infringement of that person's rights that it can only very exceptionally be justified.

Although Lord Windlesham, the chair of the Parole Board, at least acknowledges that 'the presumption of innocence does not sit comfortably with the denial of bail',[100] he hopes to escape this dilemma by the administrative separation of the remand system from the prisons, placing the former under private management to symbolize its distinctness from the punitive institutions of the state. But stressing the distinction between 'detention' in a 'remand unit' and 'punishment' in a 'prison' not only does nothing to make the loss of liberty more tolerable, it may actually make matters worse by clouding still further the judiciary's and the public's perception of the seriousness of imprisoning the innocent. The likelihood that private contractors would go out of their way to emphasize the mildness of their regimes further exacerbates this danger.

Finally, it is certainly questionable whether the distinction currently being drawn between remand facilities and mainstream prisons will last. Edward Gardiner, for example, has made it perfectly clear (in the *File on 4* programme on BBC Radio 4 on 14 November 1988) that he could see no reason in principle why the experiment with private remand facilities should not, if successful, be carried over to other prisons.

Prison building

The Home Affairs Committee argued for privatization as a means to add 'a new dimension of urgency and flexibility to the prison building programme'. They also claimed that it would dramatically improve prison design, although most prison design work is in fact done by private firms already.[101] Don Hutto of CCA, addressing a meeting of British parliamentarians in February 1988, claimed to have planned, financed, designed and built a prison in ten months.[102] This is certainly a lot quicker than the seven years or so it typically takes in England; but the comparative performance of public and private agencies in the context of the American system of planning and public finance cannot be taken as a reliable guide to how they would perform here. For example, according to the Home Secretary the first two years out of the seven 'are spent discussing proposals with local authorities and local residents'.[103] Local authorities have few legal powers over land owned by government departments; but formal planning procedures would apply to land owned or leased by a private company. The Home Secretary has stated categorically that 'We would not solve any of the planning problems of new prisons and remand centres by privatizing.'[104] Despite this apparent scepticism, in April 1988 the new Home Office Prisons Building Board issued an invitation to the private sector to submit outline proposals for building new urban remand centres and open prisons, stressing that 'The Home Office is particularly interested in securing the early availability of the new accommodation.'[105]

It would require a complex and lengthy analysis to determine what lessons if any could be learnt from the American private sector's approach to prison construction. We do not propose to undertake such an exercise because, like most of the penal lobby in Britain, we are opposed to building new prisons, on the grounds that the country already has more prison space than any reasonable penal policy would require and that the money could be far better spent in other ways.[106]

In any case, even if the private sector were to take a greater role in prison construction, it hardly follows that it should also manage the prisons it builds. The Green Paper hints at a possible rationale for combining the two roles when it suggests that contractors who were responsible for both building and management might develop 'design solutions which took account of particular modes of operation, and vice versa' (para. 80). Of course, any kind of specialist building needs to be designed in close consultation with its eventual users; but that does not mean that architect and client have to be one and the same firm.

Prison industry

The 'factories with fences' model of prisons has its adherents in Britain as well as the United States. The most enthusiastic are Hall and Woodhead, who appear to see the revitalization of prison industries as a virtual panacea for the problems of the penal system. A more carefully thought-out approach is offered by McConville and Hall Williams in their pamphlet for the Tawney Society, the 'think tank' of the old Social Democratic Party. They lay down a rigorous set of conditions that would have to be met for private enterprise in prisons to be viable and acceptable. Industry must be able to make as great a profit in prisons as it could elsewhere. The prisoners employed should be volunteers, hired and fired by the managers of the enterprise. They would receive 'a reasonable market wage and better than average living conditions', but would have to pay for their keep, the upkeep of their dependants and any court orders outstanding against them. Industrial prisons would need to be specially designed. A trained, stable, labour force would be needed, so only medium- or long-term prisoners would be eligible. The prison service would have to guarantee to cooperate with the company for several years. Unions would need to be reassured that 'neither through government subsidy or less than market wages would labour costs undercut the market'. The enterprise should be a new one, not a replacement for one employing free labour, and should preferably create some jobs for non-prisoners. And, ninth but not least, prisoners should be able to join a union, though they might be excluded from some union activities for security reasons.[107]

It is hard to deny that if all these conditions could be met the result would be an improvement on the compulsory, non-unionized drudgery and derisory wages which prevail in those prison workshops which currently operate at all. But it seems unlikely (for the reasons discussed in Chapter 2) that more than a handful of companies would find such an operation worthwhile or that more than a small elite of prisoners would benefit. There is something strangely anachronistic, in present economic circumstances, about attempting to mimic in prisons the working conditions of a declining industrial proletariat. This is not to suggest, however, that providing constructive activities for prisoners is unimportant or that prison industry can never be a site for progressive penal practice. On the contrary, we take seriously the argument that prison industries have the potential for redefining social relationships inside the prison away from their traditional hierarchical norm; and the idea, recently put forward in Australia, for the creation of small-scale prison cooperatives is one which, in another context, we would be more than happy to explore.[108]

Prison services

As in the United States, the privatization of prison services is less controversial than outright private management; but it has aroused considerable opposition. A number of services are already contracted out in many prisons, including hair cutting, window cleaning, refuse collection and pest control.[109] At Alma Dettingen, a converted barracks which during 1988 was run by the army as a temporary prison to relieve overcrowding, a private contractor provided the prisoners' food. The POA sees the privatization of further services, including catering and the provision of prison canteens (i.e. shops) as a major threat to its members' interests, and also as a threat to security, since it argues that the canteens, for example, are an important source of intelligence about drugs and other illicit goods coming into the prisons.

This is – for obvious reasons – a difficult argument to assess and it would also be rather a strange one for the Left to support. One of the guiding principles of the penal lobby in recent years has been King and Morgan's concept of 'normalization', aimed at minimizing the differences between prisons and the outside world.[110] As Morgan and King themselves have pointed out, their view that 'services within prison should be provided by the same commercial, voluntary or statutory agencies which normally provide them within the community' has important implications for the privatization debate:

> Contracting out in this sense could be to a variety of agencies: health to the
> NHS; libraries to local authority library services; workshops to local firms

or NACRO; . . . mother and baby units to one of the child care agencies. Some services might be provided for profit, others not.[111]

So why not, as Stephen Shaw of the PRT suggests, extend the principle to Marks and Spencer running the prison canteen?[112] In the view of the prisoners' organization PROP, privatizing canteens or catering does not raise 'any issue worth arguing about, nor can we see prisoners being either better or worse off for having their food dished up by Sir Charles Forte in one of his more downmarket moods'.[113] While we agree that private catering or retail services are not objectionable as a matter of general principle, we do not support policies of cutting costs by replacing relatively well paid, unionized workers with what would probably be very badly paid, non-unionized ones. Moreover, such a change could have at least two adverse effects on prisoners. First, they could lose the training opportunities provided by the catering service; and, secondly, the profits of prison canteens are at present paid into a 'general purpose fund' which can be used for such things as improved recreation facilities for prisoners; this income could be lost if the profit went to an outside company.[114]

Rather more fundamental concerns are raised by the possible privatization of services concerned directly with security, such as escorting prisoners to and from court, a duty which both the Green Paper and HM Chief Inspector of Prisons have suggested could be undertaken by private security firms.[115] Since we are dealing here with staff who may come into violent conflict with prisoners, very firm assurances would be needed about their training and accountability and such staff would certainly need to be better trained, and better paid, than the average security guard.[116] Moreover the prison governors seem to have a reasonable point when they say that the tense situation of escorting a prisoner to and from court may be better handled by an officer who already knows the individual concerned.[117]

Morgan and King's suggestion that mother and baby units could be contracted out to (presumably charitable) child care agencies is an interesting one. It could be argued that outside agencies would be less likely than prison staff to impose the kind of unduly rigid discipline which characterizes such units at present.[118] But contracting out of welfare services is unlikely to be beneficial if, as seems all too probable, it is done primarily with a view to saving money. Here, as in the case of the American non-profit sector, the spectre of 'commodification' – the reduction of welfare to a commodity to be purchased as cheaply as possible – raises its head.

Prisons and the voluntary sector

Morgan and King do not see the voluntary sector's role as limited to the provision of prison services, but suggest that a whole prison might be turned over to a voluntary organization such as NACRO. Jeremy Handley, one of the Conservative members of the Home Affairs Committee, made a similar suggestion when NACRO gave evidence.[119] NACRO itself has repeatedly, and indignantly, rejected the idea. There is no shortage of American and British precedents for voluntary organizations running custodial institutions; but we are unable to see the merit of a proposal which would merely, as in the case of the Victorian reformatories, lend a spurious veneer of benevolence to institutions whose purposes are anything but benevolent.

Morgan and King are quite right, however, to take opponents of privatization to task for failing to extend the debate to non-profit making private bodies. As we have seen, the argument advanced by the Howard League, NACRO and others against the state's 'abdicating responsibility' for the punishment of offenders would logically apply to non-custodial penalties administered by the voluntary sector, though clearly no such implication is intended. Of the other arguments against privatization, those concerned with profits and pecuniary vested interests clearly do not apply with the same force to voluntary bodies – though we saw in the case of the reformatories and approved schools how even a charity can acquire a vested interest in keeping up the number of its clients. However, the argument that measures which rely on the direct use of force need to be subject to particularly close supervision, and that this requirement conflicts with the flexibility, cheapness and freedom from bureaucracy that privatization is intended to achieve, applies to any private institution at the 'deep end' of the penal continuum, whether profit making or not.

CONCLUSION

It should be clear from the above that we have a number of ethical and political objections to the private management of prisons and we also have serious anxieties about the effects on prisoners and staff of privatizing prison services. Where we part company from many opponents of privatization is over the idea that there is somehow a fixed and immutable relationship between punishment and the state. Not only does such a premise ignore the long tradition of privately run penal institutions in Britain, it also ignores or confuses crucial issues about the role of the voluntary or non-profit sector in the penal system. These issues, which we shall explore in the next chapter, are among the most interesting and politically significant questions thrown up by the privatization debate.

NOTES

1. P. Haagen, 'Eighteenth-century English society and the debt law', in S. Cohen and A. Scull (eds), *Social Control and the State*, Blackwell, Oxford, 1985.
2. S. McConville, *A History of English Prison Administration*, Vol. I, RKP, London, 1981, Chapter 3; S. Spitzer and A. Scull, 'Social control in historical perspective: from private to public responses to crime', in D. F. Greenberg (ed.), *Corrections and Punishment*, Sage, Beverly Hills and London, 1977, pp. 272–4.
3. M. Ignatieff, *A Just Measure of Pain: The Penitentiary in the Industrial Revolution*, Macmillan, London, 1978, p. 113.
4. *Op. cit.*, note 2, McConville, pp. 247–8.

5. G. de Beaumont and A. de Tocqueville, *On the Penitentiary System of the United States*, Southern Illinois University Press, 1964, p. 131; G. Rusche and O. Kirchheimer, *Punishment and Social Structure*, Columbia University Press, New York, 1939, pp. 110–13.

6. D. Melossi and M. Pavarini, *The Prison and the Factory*, Macmillan/Società editrice il Mulino, London/Bologna, 1981, p. 61. The work of G. L. Chesterton (see Chapter 3, note 1 above) is a case in point.

7. *Op. cit.*, note 2, McConville, pp. 350–51.

8. The evidence of Mr James Duncan to the Departmental Committee on Prisons, *Parl. Papers* 1895, LVI, pp. 205–13, provides a fascinating account of prison industries before and after centralization. The statistics on mat-making are at Q4373.

9. *Ibid.*, para. 57.

10. Departmental Committee on the Employment of Prisoners, *Parl. Papers* 1933–4, XV, p. 105, para. 141.

11. *Ibid.*

12. Committee of Public Accounts, *Prison Industry Losses*, 1985–86 HC 160, HMSO, London, 1986.

13. Written answer by the Home Secretary, *House of Commons Official Report* 31 October 1984, cols 987–8.

14. L. Radzinowicz and R. Hood, *A History of English Criminal Law*, Vol. 5: *The Emergence of Penal Policy*, Stevens, London, 1986, pp. 149, 158, 174.

15. Select Committee on Criminal and Destitute Juveniles, Minutes of Evidence, *Parl. Papers* 1852, VII, p. 1, Q822.

16. *Ibid.*

17. *Op. cit.*, note 14, p. 175.

18. In Scotland, industrial schools were established earlier but initially had no powers of detention; their subsequent absorbtion into the penal system could be taken as an early example of the process of 'publicization' discussed in Chapter 5 below. See O. Checkland, *Philanthropy in Victorian Scotland*, John Donald, Edinburgh, 1980.

19. Report of the Departmental Committee on Reformatory and Industrial Schools, *Parl. Papers* 1896, XLV, p. 1, at para. 12.

20. *Report of the Committee on Children and Young Persons*, 1959–60, Cmnd 1191, para. 415.

21. *Op. cit.*, note 14, pp. 183–202.

22. Report of the Select Committee on Reformatory and Industrial Schools, *Parl. Papers* 1884, XLV, pp. 13–14.

23. *Op. cit.*, note 19, para. 201.

24. *Ibid.* On the other aspects of this report see A. Rutherford, *Growing Out of Crime*, Penguin, Harmondsworth, 1986, pp. 39–42.

25. Report of the Departmental Committee on Reformatory and Industrial Schools, *Parl. Papers* 1913, XXXIX.

26. J. Carlebach, *Caring for Children in Trouble*, Routledge, London, 1970.

27. G. Rose, *Schools for Young Offenders*, Tavistock, London, 1967, pp. 108–9.

28. The Curtis Committee on *The Care of Children*, *Parl. Papers* 1946–7, X, para. 283 considered that the role of the Home Office was such that the distinction between charitable approved schools and those run by local authorities was no longer significant.

29. Report of the Committee of Enquiry into the Conduct of Standon Farm Approved School, *Parl. Papers* 1947, XIV, p. 461.

30. *Ibid.*, and also the Report on the Disturbances at the Carlton Approved School, *Parl. Papers* 1959/60, XIX, p. 625.
31. Administration of Punishment at Court Lees Approved School, *Parl. Papers* 1966–67, XXVI, p. 149.
32. An early and outstanding exception was the highly innovative Little Commonwealth, which for 15 months in 1917–18 enjoyed the status of a certified reformatory school. See D. W. Wills, *Homer Lane: A Biography*, Allen and Unwin, London, 1964.
33. *Op. cit.*, note 26, pp. 103, 111–13, 137, 153–5.
34. S. Millham, R. Bullock and P. Cherrett, *After Grace – Teeth*, Human Context, London, 1975, pp. 53–5.
35. For an absorbing but partisan account of one such transformation, see D. W. Wills, *Spare the Child*, Penguin, Harmondsworth, 1970.
36. *Op. cit.*, note 34, p. 50.
37. *Ibid.*, pp. 66, 99; *op. cit.*, note 26, pp. 116, 162.
38. T. Hopkins, 'Child care at a profit', *New Society*, 19 April 1979, pp. 135–6.
39. D. Berridge, 'Private children's homes', *British Journal of Social Work*, 14, 1984, pp. 347–66. Berridge's survey specifically excluded CHEs.
40. M. Knapp, 'Private children's homes', *Policy and Politics*, 15, 4, 1987, pp. 221–34.
41. J. Laurance, 'Is big business moving into caring?' *New Society*, 63, 1983, pp. 221–4.
42. *Op. cit.*, note 40, p. 225.
43. B. Hudson, *Justice Through Punishment*, Macmillan, London, 1987, pp. 155–6.
44. *Checkpoint: The Mindbenders*, 18 October 1984, BBC transcript. See also the book by the presenter and researcher of the programme, R. Cook and T. Tate, *What's Wrong With Your Rights?*, Methuen, London, 1988.
45. 'Consenting to behaviour modification', *Childright*, 21, 1985.
46. *Op. cit.*, note 24.
47. S. d'Orey, *Immigration Prisoners: A Forgotten Minority*, Runnymede Trust, London, 1984; House of Commons, *Fifteenth Report of the Expenditure Committee: The Reduction of Pressure on the Penal System: Minutes of Evidence*, HMSO, 1978.
48. D. Campbell, 'New prison for immigrants?' *New Statesman*, 1 June 1984.
49. Written answer, *House of Commons Official Report*, 30 March 1987, cols. 344–5.
50. Written answer, *House of Commons Official Report*, 16 May 1988, cols. 312–16. *Guardian*, 2 May 1987.
51. *City Limits*, 18–25 June 1987, p. 8; 'Home Office shame at Harwich', *Searchlight*, 147, September 1987, p. 19; information from Women in Prison.
52. S. Braden, 'Dead end', *Guardian*, 8 August 1987.
53. S. Shaw, *Conviction Politics*, Fabian Society, London, 1987; 'Private prisons: who guards the Securicor guards?' *AMBOV Quarterly*, July 1985, p. 4.
54. *Op. cit.*, note 47, House of Commons, Qq.1776–8.
55. Immigration and Nationality Department, *Annual Report 1985*, HMSO, London, 1986; Written answer, *House of Commons Official Report*, 14 April 1983, col. 221.
56. *Op. cit.*, note 47, d'Orey, p. 26.
57. Cf. PROP, 'Private prisons: by appointment to HM the Queen', *Abolitionist*, 23, 1987, pp. 23–4.
58. In an interview with Paul Barker of the *Sunday Telegraph*, 4 October 1987.

59. Howard League, in Home Affairs Committee, *The State and Use of Prisons: Minutes of Evidence*, 1986–7, HC 35-II, p. 94.
60. Minutes of the Group's meeting on 1 March 1988.
61. *Op. cit.*, note 59, p. 95; and see above, p. 51.
62. H. Gerth and C. Wright Mills, *From Max Weber*, Routledge, London, 1970, p. 78. Weber goes on: 'Specifically, at the present time, the right to use physical force is ascribed to other institutions or individuals only to the extent that the State permits it.'
63. C. H. Logan, *Privatizing Prisons: The Moral Case*, ASI Research, London, 1987, p. 1. (This is a slightly abridged version of 'The propriety of proprietary prisons', *Federal Probation*, September 1987, pp. 35–9.)
64. P. Gilroy and J. Sim, 'Law, order and the state of the left', in P. Scraton (ed.), *Law, Order and the Authoritarian State*, Open University Press, Milton Keynes, 1987.
65. Home Affairs Committee, *Fourth Report, Contract Provision of Prisons*, 1986–7, HC 291, para. 14.
66. P. Young, *The Prison Cell*, ASI Research, London, 1987, p. 34.
67. N. Christie, *Limits to Pain*, Martin Robertson, Oxford, 1982 and 'Some criteria for evaluating penal systems', paper delivered at the European Group for the Study of Deviance and Social Control, Vienna, 1987. On the place of moral arguments of this kind in critical criminology, see also W. de Haan, 'Fuzzy morals and flakey politics', *Journal of Law and Society*, 27, 3, 1987, pp. 321–33.
68. S. Shaw, *Conviction Politics*, Fabian Society, London, 1988, p. 21.
69. Quoted in the *Morning Star*, 28 March 1987.
70. D. J. Palumbo, 'Privatization and the corrections policy', *Policy Studies Review*, 5, 1986, pp. 598–606; I. P. Robbins, 'Privatization of corrections: defining the issues', *Judicature*, 69, 1986, pp. 325–31.
71. Labour Party Policy Directorate, *Company Donations to the Conservative Party and other Political Organizations*, London, 1987.
72. BBC Radio 4, *File on 4*, 14 November 1988.
73. Adam Smith Institute, *Omega Report: Justice Policy*, London, 1984, p. 62; Young, *op. cit.*, note 66, p. 4.
74. *Op. cit.*, note 63; POA in Home Affairs Committee, *Minutes of Evidence*, 1986–87, HC 35-II.
75. Prison Act 1952, s. 8.
76. P. Carlen, *Women's Imprisonment*, Routledge, London, 1983, pp. 112–15.
77. R. King, 'Control in prisons', in M. Maguire, J. Vagg and R. Morgan (eds), *Accountability and Prisons*, Tavistock, London, 1985, p. 4.
78. See, for example, *The Roof Comes Off: The Report of the Independent Inquiry Into Protests at Peterhead Prison*, Gateway Exchange, Edinburgh, 1987; G. Coggan and M. Walker, *Frightened for My Life*, Fontana, London, 1982.
79. J. Lea, R. Matthews and J. Young, *Law and Order Five Years On*, Middlesex Polytechnic, Enfield, 1987, p. 53; P. Lerman, 'Child welfare, the private sector and community-based corrections', *Crime and Delinquency*, 30, 1, 1984. See also I. Schwartz, M. Jackson-Beeck and R. Anderson, 'The hidden system of juvenile control', *Crime and Delinquency*, 30, 3, 1984, which points to the over-representation of girls in private institutions.
80. M. Taylor and K. Pease, 'Private prison and penal purpose', in R. Matthews (ed.), *Privatizing Criminal Justice*, Sage, London, forthcoming.
81. R. Hall and N. Woodhead, 'Privatizing prisons', paper presented to the Politics Association, 1985.

82. See the forceful evidence of the prison governors to the Home Affairs Committee, *op. cit.*, note 59, p. 60. On financial accountability within the Home Office, see also *op. cit.*, note 76.

83. D. Saunders Wilson, 'Privatization and the future of imprisonment', *Prison Service Journal*, April 1986, pp. 7–9 (also published as 'Profitable prisons', *Openmind*, 20, April/May 1986).

84. *Op. cit.*, note 63.

85. When questioned on this point in the Prison Reform Trust's debate on 'Privatization and the prisons', Professor Taylor did not give any specific examples.

86. See *op. cit.*, note 43.

87. D. Downes, *Contrasts in Tolerance*, Clarendon, Oxford, 1988, p. 116.

88. J. Vagg, R. Morgan and M. Maguire, 'Introduction', in *op. cit.*, note 7.

89. I. Robbins, *The Legal Dimensions of Private Incarceration*, American Bar Association, Washington, 1988, pp. 141–8.

90. The *Daily Telegraph* reported on 12 February 1988 that the Home Office's legal advisers had concluded that new legislation would be needed. Section 3 of the 1952 Act also has ambiguous implications for privatization.

91. J. E. Thomas, 'Dangers for prisoners when the state stops guarding the guards', *Independent*, 28 July 1987.

92. M. Ryan, *The Politics of Penal Reform*, Longman, Harlow, 1983, Chapter 5.

93. J. Boyle, *The Pain of Confinement*, Canongate, Edinburgh, 1984.

94. Prison Reform Trust, *Prison Medicine*, London, 1985; RAP, 'Prison education', *Abolitionist*, 13, 1983.

95. G. Richardson, 'The case for prisoners' rights', in *op. cit.*, note 77.

96. R. Matthews, 'Taking realist criminology seriously', *Contemporary Crises*, 11, 1987, p. 383.

97. See, e.g. K. Russell, 'Privatization of prisons', *New Law Journal*, 27 February 1987, pp. 193–4; *op. cit.*, note 73.

98. See the First Report from the House Affairs Committee, 1983–4, *Remands in Custody*, HC 252 and the series of *Remand Project Papers* published by the Prison Reform Trust.

99. Quoted in *Remands in Custody – some Facts and Figures*, NACRO Briefing, 1988.

100. Lord Windlesham, 'Punishment and prevention: the inappropriate prisoners', *Criminal Law Review*, 1988, pp. 140–51.

101. Home Affairs Committee, *Contract Provision of Prisons*, para. 9; speech by Lord Caithness quoted in *NACRO News Digest*, 47, November 1987.

102. Parliamentary All Party Penal Affairs Group, *Minutes*, 16 February 1988.

103. Oral answer, *House of Commons Official Report*, 2 April 1987, col. 1211.

104. *Ibid.*, 30 March 1988, col. 1098.

105. Quoted in *NACRO News Digest*, August 1988.

106. This case is well argued in the Prison Reform Trust's Evidence to the Home Affairs Committee, and by A. Rutherford, *Prisons and the Process of Justice*, Oxford University Press, Oxford, 1986. The novelist Alice Thomas Ellis, in *The Times*, 16 September 1987, predicts that the new prisons 'will be filled almost immediately. I am familiar with this syndrome, having the same problem with books and bookshelves. . . . I don't believe private prisons would achieve anything except incarcerating a yet more excessive proportion of the population.'

107. S. McConville and E. Hall Williams, *Crime and Punishment: A Radical Rethink*, Tawney Society, London, 1985, pp. 31–7. The Adam Smith Institute has also taken

up the cause of private industry in prisons: *Making Prison Work*, ASI, London, 1988.

108. We are grateful to David Brown for making this point.
109. Written answer, *House of Commons Official Report*, 26 July 1985, col. 811.
110. R. King and R. Morgan, *The Future of the Prison System*, Gower, Aldershot, 1980.
111. R. Morgan and R. King, 'Profiting from prison', *New Society*, 23 October 1987, pp. 21–2.
112. S. Shaw, 'Privatization and penal reform', *Prison Report*, 1, 1987.
113. *Op. cit.*, note 57.
114. Our thanks to Sally Swift for pointing this out to us.
115. Home Office, *Private Sector Involvement in the Remand System*, Cm 434, 1988, paras 32–42; HM Chief Inspector Of Prisons, *Annual Report for 1986*, HMSO, London, 1988.
116. A survey by the GMB union found that the average pay of security guards was less than £2 an hour for a 60-hour week. D. Felton, 'Police chiefs call for curbs on security companies', *Independent*, 19 August 1988.
117. *Op. cit.*, note 59, Home Affairs Committee, Q173.
118. A. Mama, M. Mars and P. Stevenson, *Breaking the Silence*, London Strategic Policy Unit, 1987, pp. 124–34.
119. *Op. cit.*, note 111; *op. cit.*, note 59, Home Affairs Committee, Q91.

CHAPTER 5

The shallow end:
the public, the private
and the social

We regard the role of the voluntary sector, and particularly its role at the 'soft' or 'shallow end' of the penal complex, as one of the major unresolved issues in privatization debate despite, or rather because of, the fact that it has been largely uncontroversial. Though there are those who believe that all forms of punishment should be a statutory responsibility,[1] most critics of privatization see it as desirable, or at least acceptable, for the voluntary sector to play a part in administering non-custodial sanctions. While supporters of privatization are happy to refer selectively to non-profit agencies as precedents, their opponents are equally happy to regard such agencies as entirely distinct from private prison contractors without thinking through exactly what the distinction is.

It is certainly not our intention to suggest that these two forms of private involvement in the penal system are indistinguishable. On the contrary, it will become clear as this chapter progresses that the political and theoretical issues they raise are in many ways quite different. But we have also seen, particularly with reference to American and British juvenile institutions, that the boundaries are by no means tightly drawn. Some voluntary agencies differ very little from their profit making counterparts and some of the facilities they provide bear more than a passing resemblance to prisons. Admittedly this blurring of boundaries is much more pronounced in the USA than in Britain, where with the exception of children's homes the soft end of the system has so far been the exclusive preserve of non-profit making agencies; but this may soon change, as we shall see.

We shall return to the question of where the limits of acceptable private involvement should be drawn in Chapter 6. In this chapter we want to look more closely at the present role of the voluntary sector, and the potential role of the commercial sector, at the shallow end of the British penal system.

THE VOLUNTARY SECTOR AND THE WELFARE STATE

The word 'privatization' is too simple to describe adequately the evolving relationship between the voluntary sector and the penal system. Rather, what has happened historically, and is arguably happening now, is that the public and the private have become increasingly intertwined. Around the turn of the century the state became increasingly involved in subsidizing, regulating and co-ordinating the work of a range of voluntary agencies in the field of penal policy and of social welfare generally.[2] As Donzelot puts it,

> philanthropy began a new phase of its career – less spectacular, perhaps, but more serene, as it was now housed in the body of the State . . . with agents mandated by public authorities and supported by the administrative and disciplinary powers of the State.

This interpenetration of state power and private philanthropy was part of the process which brought into being the new 'sector' which Donzelot terms 'the social' (the realm of social work, social welfare, etc.): a sector which straddles and blurs the old boundaries between the public and the private, the penal and the 'assistantial'.[3]

The early development of probation and after-care in England typified this process. The Police Court Missions, who provided the majority of probation officers from 1908 to 1936, and the Discharged Prisoners Aid Societies responsible for after-care, submitted to a considerable degree of state regulation, in return for which the state provided them both with funding and with a new kind of power over their clients, backed by the threat of imprisonment (in the case of probation) of with being compelled to report to the police (in the case of ex-prisoners).[4] The fact that the Missionaries represented a private, religious organization, rather than the state, was thought to make it easier for them to win acceptance as 'friends' of their clients, intermediaries who would plead with the courts to show mercy to those offenders who expressed willingness to reform. In practice, the relationship between the Police Court Missions and the state was an uneasy one; there were numerous administrative and financial problems and the evangelical outlook of the Missions' leadership was at odds with the more 'scientific' spirit favoured by the Home Office and by many probation officers. These tensions led to the reorganization of probation as a state controlled, professionalized service in 1936; but after-care remained in the voluntary sector until 1963.[5]

There are several aspects of these early forms of voluntary involvement which remain relevant today. First, there is the way in which charitable workers were used to give supervision a relatively informal, benevolent image and to avoid some of the stigma associated with supervision by the police. Then there is the paradoxical form of power, characteristic of many 'alternatives to custody' whether statutory or voluntary, which probation officers exercised in the very act of trying, in all good faith, to shield their clients from the full power of the state.[6] The power of procuring mercy may be scarcely less awesome than the power of dispensing justice. And finally, there is the dilemma faced by the Missions, once they had been co-opted into the criminal justice system, between accommodating to the demands of the system or remaining true to their original ideals at the cost, ultimately, of their semi-official status. The ideals were essentially conservative, but the dilemma is familiar to present day radicals.

These themes of power, co-option and outward benevolence recur in the accounts of privatization at the soft end of the system put forward (rather sketchily) by Stan Cohen[7] and, with much greater sophistication, in Ericson, McMahon and Evans' analysis of the Canadian privatization debate, a debate which has been primarily concerned with voluntary rather than for profit involvement in the penal system. Ericson *et al.* argue that this form of privatization

> allows for the *apparent* decentralization of control of offenders, community involvement and distancing from the state. In effect, however, it secures 'publicization': centralized control of non-state agencies through the conditions of contract and attendant monitoring and auditing functions.[8]

The effect of such 'publicization' is that both the voluntary agency and state gain in power, while more and more people are caught in the expanding 'net' of social control (a trend exemplified by the rapid growth of privately managed community service schemes in Ontario).[9] Ericson *et al.* note that some people in the major Canadian voluntary agencies are unhappy about their increasing dependence on government contracts, which they see as imposing an overtly controlling role on them at the expense of their original, reforming, objectives. But such objections, argue Ericson *et al.*, miss the point that these agencies are already a part of 'the social', engaged just as much as state agencies in the business of control. Moreover their activities in campaigning for reform are perfectly compatible with this role, since the system needs such reformers to create the appearance of change while really changing nothing. Shifting the boundaries of public and private 're-forms' the system in just this way.

Clearly this is a thoroughly depressing analysis, which offers little comfort to either supporters or opponents of greater voluntary sector involvement. We believe that, although Ericson *et al.*'s argument contains an important degree of truth (and may be more true of Canada than of Britain),[10] it is altogether too pessimistic. More specifically, it shares a major flaw of Cohen's work (and much else in the same vein), in that it dismisses far too lightly the resistance of some of the personnel in both the voluntary and statutory sectors to the very extension of control which these authors are so worried about; a resistance which we shall argue is crucial to understanding the ambiguous politics of the voluntary sector.

But before returning to this theme, we want to consider why it is that we seem now to be witnessing a renaissance of interest in the voluntary sector, not only in the penal system but more generally. Is it part of a 'return to Victorian (or Edwardian) values'? Or does it herald a more flexible, decentralized way of administering welfare – and punishment too?

While there are indeed parallels between the voluntary sector's role in the 1900s and the present, there is also an important contrast: today it is not merely the individual or the family, but the community, that is the object of intervention. Whereas voluntary agencies in probation and after-care (and, half a century earlier, in Mary Carpenter's reformatories) were thought to be able to establish a kind of relationship with individuals that would be difficult or impossible for officials of the state, from the late 1960s onwards one of the main attractions of voluntary agencies – and also of decentralized structures within the statutory sector – has been the desire to establish a closer relationship with that elusive and indefinable entity, the community.[11]

One of the most notable manifestations of this enthusiasm for 'community' in social policy was the development in the late 1960s and early 1970s of 'community work', an initiative which had as one of its main objectives the reduction of juvenile delinquency. Although community work can be traced back to the Victorian settlement movement, its rapid expansion in this period owed much to the American 'war on poverty', and to the 'discovery' that poverty still existed in Britain in spite of the post-war welfare state.[12] In essence, community workers are employed by the state (usually at local government level) or by voluntary organizations to help the residents of particular, mainly poor, neighbourhoods to identify their common needs and then to take some form of action together to meet them and, through this process, to develop a strengthened sense of 'community'.

The original impetus behind community work, from the Home Office and other government departments, was based largely on notions of social pathology; on the assumption that, if the poor remained poor despite the welfare state, it must be as a result of their own inadequacy or incompetence. This kind of thinking was quickly rejected by most community workers, and gave place, in official circles, to what Cynthia Cockburn has termed the 'social planning' approach, which aimed to improve communication between the local state and the population it served.[13] Many community workers moved beyond this approach to a more radical view in which the state itself and, for some, the capitalist system it served, were seen as the problem. Many professionals in community work and related fields were inspired by the ideas of the New Left – that heady brew of counterculture and Marxism – to develop alternative, participatory political structures outside the formal apparatus of 'bourgeois democracy'. Often they chose to work in the voluntary sector, believing that this offered them greater autonomy than working directly for the state.[14] Even within the statutory sector, community work projects often attained a quite remarkable degree of autonomy and 'a relationship with government more similar to that of Shelter or the Child Poverty Action Group than that of a statutory agency'.[15]

These developments within community work, and Cockburn's analysis of them in particular, illustrate how some agencies can be *both* part of a strategy for increasing the state's penetration of the 'community' *and* the sites for real oppositional struggles. Although the independence of government funded voluntary organizations has been noticeably eroded since Mrs Thatcher came to power (for example the Community Projects Foundation, a community work organization which also works with young offenders, was warned in 1983 to control the 'political activities' of some of its staff), many small, local projects can still enjoy considerable autonomy, if only because it would be too costly to monitor them closely.'[16]

While the more radical strand of community work has, as we shall see, directly influenced several projects within and around the criminal justice system, particularly those working with young offenders, the 'social planning' approach can be seen as the precursor of 'welfare pluralism', the perspective which dominates the current debate on the role of the voluntary sector in social policy. Welfare pluralism, like community work, seeks to remedy what it sees as the bureaucratic remoteness of the welfare state, its insensitivity to the needs of the people it serves. The New Right's attacks on the welfare state have lent added urgency to this concern, which is also reflected in the 'decentralization' policies of some Labour councils.[17]

To put very simply what we take to be the political crux of the matter, welfare pluralists defend welfare without defending the welfare state, at least in its present form. They point out that welfare services can be, and are, delivered by voluntary organizations, 'informal caring networks' (a phrase which often seems to be a euphemism for unpaid female labour) and commercial enterprises, as well as by the state. While conceding that many people are dissatisfied with the welfare state bureaucracy, and with good reason, they argue that the response to that dissatisfaction should not be to cut back welfare spending, but to channel the state's resources through different organizational structures. The voluntary sector, in particular, is seen as potentially a more decentralized and participatory way of delivering welfare services. As in the 'social planning' approach to community work, the aim is to involve 'communities' more in articulating their needs and in planning the use of state resources to meet them.

It is not surprising that a large part of the voluntary sector, including the National Council of Voluntary Organizations, has embraced and championed welfare pluralism. It appears to offer the voluntary sector a way of turning the Thatcherite critique of the welfare state to its own advantage and it also provides one of those chameleon-like programmes, so familiar to penologists, which with a few modifications or changes of emphasis can blend in with almost any shade in the political spectrum. The breadth of political opinion to which the idea of enhancing the voluntary sector's role appeals is indeed remarkable: from Mrs Thatcher and her Home Secretary Douglas Hurd to socialist political theorists like Paul Hirst and John Keane.[18] (Hirst and Keane, however, are talking about the role the voluntary sector could play in a much more egalitarian and democratic society, not offering 'active citizenship' as a *substitute* for greater equality and democracy.) But despite all this excitement on the ideological front it remains true, as Norman Johnson points out, that since the advent of welfare pluralism there has been 'precious little expansion of the voluntary sector, but . . . a very rapid expansion, in nearly all welfare states, of the commercial sector'.[19]

Probably the most significant change in the position of the voluntary sector under Mrs Thatcher, as Beresford and Croft suggest in their critique of welfare pluralism, has been in the source and nature of its funding: 'while local government has had less and less resources to put into voluntary organizations, central government has been putting much more in through highly regulated and regulating bodies, most notably the Manpower Services Commission [MSC]'.[20] At this point our history comes full circle, for one of the main beneficiaries of the MSC's largesse has been none other than the former National Association of Discharged Prisoners' Aid Societies, now known as the National Association for the Care and Resettlement of Offenders (NACRO). In 1987/88 the MSC funded Community Programme schemes run by NACRO had a budget of £79 million and provided 16,188 places for long-term unemployed people, of whom about half had 'a record of offending'. In addition, NACRO's New Careers Training Agency ran 35 MSC funded Youth Training Schemes, aimed primarily at young offenders.[21] Diana Robbins' description of one such scheme confirms Beresford and Croft's view of the MSC:

> taking the funding at all involves them in a degree of MSC scrutiny which the staff of this project is able to handle, but finds unreasonable. The success of community schemes funded by the MSC depends to a great extent on the personality of the MSC link-officer assigned to them, and this – particularly if it is combined with monitoring by a sponsoring organization – can be a 'terrible burden' on some of them.[22]

In the course of 1988, the MSC was first re-named the Training Commission and then abolished. It remains to be seen what impact this, and the new Employment Training programme, will have on the voluntary sector.

While it is perhaps overstating the case to call NACRO 'an executive arm of the MSC',[23] its development does look like a clear example of the 'publicization of the private', and also of the compatibility of such publicization with NACRO's other role as a reforming pressure group. We want to argue, however, that this pattern is only one among a range of possible relationships between the state and the voluntary sector and we shall illustrate this argument by looking at a number of projects which (unlike NACRO's employment schemes) are clearly within the ambit of the penal system. Our survey progresses, crudely speaking, from left to right across the political spectrum, beginning with some overtly radical projects and ending with some of the more alarming ways in which privatization (on either a commercial or a non-profit basis) could promote the extension of social control.

RADICAL ALTERNATIVES

We begin with a project of which we both have firsthand knowledge, and which, although now defunct for several years, remains an interesting example of the possibilities for radical intervention at the soft end of the system.[24] The Newham Alternatives Project (NAP) was set up in 1974 as an attempt to put into practice the ideas of its parent organization Radical Alternatives to Prison

(RAP). Earlier, RAP had outlined the type of 'community programme' which could serve as an alternative to prison: one which would 'emphasize self-help, i.e. those involved determine what is important; . . . blur the boundaries between offenders and non-offenders; [and be] concerned not just with individuals' problems of living in the community but with changing some of that community's problems'.[25] (The second point is particularly interesting; it gives something of jolt, nowadays, to find Stan Cohen having to defend NAP against criticism of its lack of blurred boundaries!)[26] In practice, however, participation in NAP was limited to people considered 'at risk' of being sent to prison.

NAP took advantage of what was then a new provision, the deferred sentence. The idea of this measure was that a judge or magistrate could postpone passing sentence to give the offender a chance to take advantage of some change in circumstances, for example an offer of employment, which might help him or her to settle down and keep within the law. NAP was to be that change in circumstances, a centre offering a range of supportive activities from literacy classes to help with making welfare claims.[27] No one was compelled to take part in any of these activities, but the possibility that doing so might help them avoid imprisonment was an important incentive. But although it was, in this sense, a part of the penal complex, NAP was explicit in its view that the existing penal apparatus as a whole was oppressive and unjust, and it aimed to communicate that view both to its 'participants' and to other local residents. For a time, at least, NAP was quite successful in maintaining this oppositional stance while attracting funding from a variety of statutory and charitable sources, including the Home Office. What eventually led to its demise was a decline in the number of deferred sentences it was able to attract, which seems to have been at least partly attributable to some of its radical practices, such as its determination never to submit a negative report on any participant. In his preface to a report on NAP, Cohen suggested that such projects were always likely to have a limited lifespan. 'But,' he added, 'to admit these limitations is not to justify doing nothing. Projects like these should be set up – then their organizers should know when to self-destruct and move (like a guerilla army) to another part of the system.'[28]

NAP was, in fact, wound up in 1980, but it was not followed by many similar 'guerrilla actions', at least in the adult penal system. There was, by this time, a growing sense of disillusion – to which Cohen's own work to some extent contributed – with the idea of emptying the prisons by creating new alternatives and also with the kind of New Left (or 'Left idealist') politics that had inspired NAP.[29] The general shift to the right in ˉBritish politics, the increasing difficulties of attracting funding and the movement away from a welfare-oriented approach to crime, have all created a less than congenial climate for such experiments.

At the same time, however, there was a growing interest among a significant minority of probation officers in developing practices consistent with socialist political principles: working with individuals in ways which, without imposing the officer's views on them, may increase their political awareness; educating the public about the realities of crime and the futility of imprisonment; resisting the trend towards more coercive forms of supervision.[30] Although they are state employees some probation officers have explored the possibilities of using the voluntary sector for radical purposes. An interesting example is Paul James' work on day centres. Some day centres operated by the probation service have very structured regimes and attendance is compulsory; others, which James prefers, are much more informal and attendance is purely voluntary and not always confined to people on probation. James points out that it is possible for a day centre to be linked to the probation service but to have its own voluntary management committee and separate funding:

> This provides greater potential for links with local groups and response to local issues than would a purely service-based resource where such contacts may be considered outside its brief. A community based centre may also offer the opportunity to work in a co-operative, non-hierarchical manner which can provide a model for socialist ways of working and organizing. The sharing of resources can bring close contact with women's groups, black organizations and trade unions.[31]

Such contacts, James suggests, may be of educational value to both sides. But he also warns (echoing Cohen's guerrilla metaphor) of the limits to the political activities which probation officers, as state employees, can undertake: 'It's no use winning a battle if you are then in no position to continue the war!'[32]

RADICAL IT

The greatest opportunities for radical experimentation in the penal system in recent years have been afforded by the development of intermediate treatment. In the words of Robert Adams and his colleagues:

> as the 1970s progressed, intermediate treatment took on – in the eyes of many people at least – much of the glamour, novelty and apparent possibilities of affecting social change that were formerly associated with community work.[33]

Intermediate treatment is a loosely defined term for measures which deal with young offenders (or young people 'at risk' of offending) outside their home environment but do not involve long-term removal from home. When it was introduced in 1969, IT was certainly not intended as a radical measure. On the contrary, it stood firmly in the tradition of penal measures which individualize the problem of crime, concentrating on offenders' supposed personal problems rather than on any social factors. To some practitioners, however, the introduction of an element of community work into IT seemed to offer a way of subverting this individualistic emphasis. In what Adams *et al.* call the 'social change' approach to IT, young people are encouraged to think about the aspects of life in their area which have led to their becoming convicted offenders and then to take action together, often in conjunction with local adults, to change those circumstances. In Nottingham, for example, young people on IT set up a group to campaign for local leisure facilities, published a magazine which expressed their views and met the local police Inspector to complain about the behaviour of some of his officers. The workers involved in these projects saw them as a way of extending the range of choices available to young people whose freedom is restricted by the combined effects of youth and poverty.[34]

The autonomy of individual projects is very important in this kind of work. Ideally, a project's 'clients', as well as its workers and local adults, should have a real say in how it is run and the project should be able to articulate a collective view independent of that of any statutory authority. Some workers also feel that being untramelled by statutory roles makes them better able to take an 'appreciative' stance towards the roles of working class youth.[35] All these considerations make voluntary status an attractive option.

Even in the voluntary sector, however, there are considerable obstacles to radical ways of working, as can be seen from Adams' thoughtful account of the Pontefract Activity Centre, a 1970s IT scheme which encouraged its participants to seek 'collective solutions to problems', such as building their own adventure playground. The centre was run by Barnardo's, one of the major child care charities, and although Adams praises their flexibility, conflict arose over

the degree to which power could be shared with any of the participants, whether young people or local adults, on issues of policy, use of resources, and project development. The indications are that locally and nationally Barnardo's were unable or unwilling to do this . . . neither parents nor children were given access to key areas of executive power in the project like decisions over the refurbishing of the building or allocation of the annual expenditure budget.[36]

Barnardo's, after all, had to take care that the project did not damage their reputation, or adopt aims in conflict with their own.[37] Adams concludes that:

the advocacy role required if hard core delinquents are to be kept in the community may necessitate the redefinition of social work relations with police and magistrates . . . such work needs to effect links between 'problem' children and their 'problem' environment, and provide them with the power to change that environment. Whilst that may be difficult for workers in the statutory agencies it may be almost as difficult for those in voluntary ones. Or perhaps a cynic would say – just as impossible.[38]

COMMUNITY IT: YOUR FLEXIBLE FRIEND

The tensions which often exist between local projects and their parent organizations[39] make it difficult to distinguish between those that are 'radical' and those that are not. What the workers at a given project think they are doing may be quite different from the pictures they present to their management committees, their parent organization or the local bench – and what the people on the receiving end make of it all may be something else again! In the literature on IT, however, there is a fairly clear distinction between those projects which portray themselves as empowering their clients and increasing their political awareness, and those which see their role as 'bridging the gap'[40] between the local state and the community at large.

In the latter perspective, which parallels the 'social planning' approach to community work, the voluntary sector can be seen to possess a number of advantages which are very similar to those claimed for it by welfare pluralism.[41] First, voluntary agencies are thought to be less likely than local authority departments

to suffer from the braking effects of bureaucratic systems and procedures. They can move faster and experiment with new approaches with far greater ease than a statutory department carrying much wider responsibilities.[42]

In other words they can lay claim to the voluntary sector's traditional virtues of innovativeness and flexibility. They may also be able to provide services (work experience courses, for instance) which do not fit easily into the brief of any one local authority department.[43]

Second, voluntary agencies, 'if their roots are genuinely local, have closer links with a community. They can quickly identify needs and problems, suggest solutions and pinpoint local people best able to help.'[44] As Cockburn suggests, the incorporation of 'community groups' into its managerial structure is one way in which the local state can gather information about the population it governs.[45] Such groups may also be thought likely to win acceptance more readily than statutory agencies (much as it was thought that police court missionaries were more likely than state-employed probation officers to be accepted as 'friends' of their clients). For example, council officers in Southwark believed that basing an IT project at a long established local charity would 'give it immediate acceptance in the neighbourhood and avoid the label associated with the statutory services'. Rather than stressing the innovative role of the voluntary sector, the local authority saw itself as taking a 'proactive' role, encouraging local charities 'to accept the changing times and find new outlets for their resources in collaborative work'.[46]

A third perceived advantage of the voluntary sector is its ability to involve local people as committee members, volunteers, etc. (though volunteers are widely used in the statutory sector as well). Such involvement is seen not simply as a source of cheap labour but as a means of educating local adults about the problems of the younger generation, problems for which the adults may be held partly responsible. For example, one of the ideas behind the formation of the Doncaster Intermediate Treatment Organization (DITO) was that:

The community often labels its own kinds before the courts do, and this may be important in understanding how delinquency is created . . . DITO's role lies in changing attitudes of local people to their kids and trying to forge better relationships between adults and young people.[47]

DITO was set up by the local social services department, which had decided to promote IT through a voluntary organization on the grounds that it would be able to perform an effective 'public relations' function and to 'involve the community' by offering free membership to anyone who was interested. Given the 'community labelling' theory on which DITO was based, it was particularly important to try to involve working class parents, but according to local probation officers:

the attitudes of adults in small neighbourhoods, their long established working class culture and resistance to change . . . [posed] problems for the engagement of volunteers in that the nature of working class lifestyles (e.g. paucity of spare time and energy) may make recruitment particularly difficult.[48]

This explanation for the well known class differentials in voluntary activity is rather too simple. The results of the 1981 General Household Survey,[49] 'while showing that those who do voluntary work are more middle aged and middle class than the population as a whole', also revealed that 'groups which might be expected to have more time available', including the unemployed, had lower than average rates of participation. Moreover, 'those in non-manual socio-economic groups were more likely to do voluntary work which was of benefit to children and teenagers', while manual workers were more likely to help the elderly – possibly their own neighbours. On the basis of these and other similar findings, and taking into account black unemployment and the number of black people in manual jobs, D. N. Thomas argues that black people are unlikely to be 'involved to any significant extent in voluntary organizations and community groups'.[50] All of which casts some doubt on the nature of the 'community' which projects like DITO are able to 'involve'.

This is not to deny that there are some voluntary organizations, for example black groups, which may genuinely enjoy a degree of legitimacy among particular sections of the population which state agencies do not. Efforts to co-opt groups like these are, as Cockburn argues of the integration of 'community groups' generally into the local state, a 'two-edged sword', bringing both dangers and opportunities to the groups concerned. If those black groups which respond to NACRO's current attempts to recruit them into the criminal justice system[51] do not tamely accept the role of managing difficult populations on the state's behalf, but rather use their position within the system to challenge the racism of the statutory agencies,[52] they may provide a further illustration of the radical possibilities of the voluntary sector.

Although belief in the superior cost-effectiveness of the voluntary sector does not appear to be a significant factor in its involvement in IT,[53] there are situations in which working with voluntary organizations is economically attractive, as is clear, for example, from Blickem and Kavanagh's account of IT in Cambridge:

[In 1979] the Social Service IT budget was £1,300 per year, and there was no likelihood that this would be increased substantially in the next 12 months. The clear choices then were either to maintain a selective and small scale IT programme or attempt to broaden its intake through the recruitment of volunteers and exploiting other resources. . . . We approached [a wide range of voluntary] organizations to determine

98

whether they could offer help either in terms of individual volunteers from their membership, use of premises, or the placement of young people in their own programmes. The response was overwhelmingly favourable . . .[54]

Trevor Locke reports that one function of Southwark Council's IT officer was to 'create new voluntary organizations to claim charitable funding thus bringing more financial resources to the borough'; but he concludes that in general 'the voluntary sector is heavily dependent on public funds and adds comparatively little cash to the IT fund'.[55] The voluntary sector can, however, attract funds from central government which are not available to local authorities. Particularly significant in this respect is the £15 million funding made available by the Department of Health and Social Security in 1983.

THE DHSS INITIATIVE

The object of this initiative was to encourage local authorities to switch resources from residential care to 'intensive' IT aimed at relatively serious offenders. To ease the 'transitional problems' which this might involve, the government offered to provide funding for new projects for two years (with partial funding for a further year), on the understanding that after this period funding would be provided by the local authority. As a means of circumventing the government's own restrictions on local government spending, the money was to be paid to voluntary organizations rather than to the authority itself; the DHSS circular announcing the scheme suggested that if a local authority could not find a suitable voluntary organization it might consider setting one up for the purpose.[56]

The circular also quoted the Government's 1980 White Paper on *Young Offenders* which emphasized the importance attached to inter-agency co-operation.[57] To further this end, projects funded under the Circular would be 'expected to be managed by a committee that includes representatives of local community interests concerned with young people'. This appears to be an endorsement of the 'voluntary inter-agency model' of IT proposed in 1980 in a report published by the National Council of Voluntary Organizations with funding from the DHSS. The report pointed out that different statutory agencies have different priorities and suggested that a scheme with an inter-agency management committee 'could provide a very useful "neutral" forum for discussion' of 'contentious issues'.[58]

By March 1986 110 IT projects had been set up under the DHSS initiative.[59] In a survey carried out by NACRO in 1985, 46 of the projects provided details of their management committees. Of these, 97 per cent (i.e. all but one) had a representative of the local social services department on the committee. The probation service was also represented on 97 per cent of committees; magistrates and their clerks on 91 per cent; the police on 84 per cent; the education service on 73 per cent; local charities on 59 per cent; the youth service on a modest 30 per cent; while only 15 per cent had any representation from local parents or other lay people. Of total committee membership 71 per cent was drawn from agencies involved in the juvenile justice system, social services representatives being the largest group, followed by magistrates and their clerks. Roughly half the projects were set up by national voluntary organizations and half by local groups, including 10 groups (out of 57 in the survey) which had been set up specifically to apply for DHSS funding.[60]

These statistics would seem to bear out Mike Nellis's view that in this area the state is 'reconstituting itself in a new guise', rather than delegating its powers to private bodies.[61] If we take seriously Francis Gladstone's statement that voluntary action is by definition 'independent of State control and voluntary organizations are essentially those established and governed by their own members without external intervention',[62] then organizations on whose governing bodies state functionaries, acting in their official capacities, are in the majority, can hardly qualify as 'voluntary' (this applies to the local inter-agency projects rather than the national charities, which often remain in effective control of their projects while the local 'management' committee performs an advisory function).[63]

We do not mean to suggest that these state functionaries constitute a monolithic bloc; on the contrary, the object of the exercise is to promote compromise between agencies whose approaches are often in conflict: a compromise by which the police issue more cautions, the magistrates pass fewer custodial sentences and social workers adopt the kind of overtly coercive approach which the police and magistrates find 'credible'. An example of this kind of bargaining at work is the Juvenile Offenders Resource Centre in Surrey, which is run by a 'partnership' between the county social services department and the Surrey Care Trust, a charity whose management committee includes senior magistrates and the chief officers of all the statutory agencies concerned with juvenile justice. This initiative was followed by a very substantial drop in custodial sentencing, from 13 per cent of convicted juveniles to somewhere between 3 and 6 per cent. The price paid by social workers is that 'A firm breach practice exists and is made clear to the courts.'[64] As Harris and Webb have shown,[65] proceedings for breach of a supervision order are generally taken with extreme reluctance, so a 'firm practice' looks like a substantial concession.

It could perhaps be argued that inter-agency cooperation is another example of a 'two-edged sword'. John Pratt, while expressing anxiety that the emphasis on inter-agency cooperation in IT may facilitate the gathering of information on individuals, also suggests that the fora provided by inter-agency meetings can be used to present information which may undermine the assumptions of some of the agencies regarding crime and punishment.[66] Unfortunately, Pratt's hope of developing a 'competing contradiction'[67] within an inter-agency framework is hardly consistent with the highly individualized approach to crime (sometimes called the 'correctional curiculum') which the new 'intensive IT' schemes typically adopt. John Pitts sees this approach as

the politically timely emergence of a revitalized Pavlovian behaviourism.
. . . If the response to young offenders is to resemble the sentence of a

court, eschew considerations of social need, and fit into a classical justice model, it must be based on a time-limited intervention which assumes that its subjects are motivated by the pursuit of pleasure and the avoidance of pain, and effect rational choices about their own behaviour. This is abominable sociology, poor psychology, but a good example of a political initiative which attempts to placate an increasingly predatory bench and government.[68]

On the other hand, if this abominable sociology succeeds in placating some predatory benches – and there is evidence that it has[69] – it could avoid quite a lot of pain for quite a number of people. Inter-agency IT may not be a two-edged sword, but it might have some value as a shield. This is an awkward point for radical critics, but it should not be ignored.

A PENAL MARKET PLACE?

Despite the emphasis which some voluntary projects place on 'selling' their activities to the government and the bench, voluntary organizations in Britain have not yet succumbed to the kind of 'commodification' we described in the American context, by which they are transformed into businesses, competing with one another to sell the most efficient possible service to the state. There are, however, some ominous signs that just such a process is beginning to occur where the delivery of welfare services is concerned. Four major charities – MIND, Help the Aged, the Spastics Society and Barnardo's – have discussed setting up a company to assist voluntary ('and possibly for-profit') bodies to bid for contracts to provide community care for elderly and disabled people, if these services are put out to tender by local authorities. The charities are said to be 'supported by' a subsidiary of the National Leasing and Finance Co.[70] If this type of relationship between the statutory, voluntary and commercial sectors becomes established in the field of welfare services, it may be only a matter of time before it spreads to the penal system.

Even if straightforward economic competition remains less significant in Britain than in the USA, there is another kind of competition which is potentially just as worrying, and that is one where voluntary, statutory and possibly commercial agencies compete with one another to 'sell' ever more coercive 'packages' of control of the courts. Pratt sees this danger as particularly acute in the juvenile justice system, where the number of offenders available for processing is beginning to decline for demographic reasons:

We can almost envisage the juvenile court being transformed into a kind of market place, where representatives of each sector and each agency come to bid against each other, as delinquency is auctioned: the winners being those who can offer the most intensive, intrusive form of supervision and surveillance for the longest period.[71]

Within the probation service, there has been considerable anxiety that the government might turn to voluntary or commercial agencies to provide forms of surveillance which many probation officers find unacceptable.[72] These fears were reinforced by a Home Office minute leaked to the National Association of Probation Officers (NAPO), which suggested that voluntary bodies might be brought in to provide tougher and more 'credible' alternatives to custody, such as 'short sharp' community service orders involving 'gruelling' work like tree felling;[73] and they were largely confirmed when the Green Paper *Punishment, Custody and the Community* was published in July 1988.

The Green Paper's central proposal is for a new sentence to be called a 'supervision and restriction order' which would enable the courts to impose a range of conditions on offenders including:

- compensation to the victim;
- community service;
- residence at a hostel or other approved place;
- prescribed activities at a day centre or elsewhere;
- curfew or house arrest;
- tracking an offender's whereabouts;
- other conditions such as staying away from particular places.

(para. 3.27)

These conditions could be combined in such a way as to add up to a deprivation of liberty virtually as severe as imprisonment. The 1988 AGM of the NAPO was unanimous in its opposition to the Green Paper's proposals, seeing them as fundamentally inconsistent with the constructive work with offenders which its members joined the probation service to do. NAPO will be hoping to repeat the success of its resistance to the curfew orders introduced by the 1982 Criminal Justice Act, which in practice have seldom been used.

The Green Paper sidesteps NAPO's objections by accepting that what it proposes is inconsistent with 'the welfare objective inherent in the present concept of the probation order' (para. 3.33) and arguing that it should therefore constitute a distinct and avowedly punitive sentence – and one which would not necessarily be administered by probation officers. The Green Paper suggests two ways in which the new sentence could be organized. One is for the probation service to supervise the order, but to contract with other agencies, including commercial and voluntary organizations, to provide some elements of it. The other is to set up a new organization which 'could contract for services from the probation service, the private or voluntary sector and perhaps for some purposes from the police or prison service' (para. 4.4). While stressing the 'great opportunities' which it offers for the probation service, and acknowledging that 'in the short term' no other organization is so well placed to supervise a new non-custodial sentence (para. 4.2), the Green Paper clearly implies that if probation officers maintain their opposition to acting as 'screws on wheels' ways will be found to implement the new sentence without them. The most likely candidates to compete with the probation service are the large national charities currently involved in work with young offenders, two of which – the Rainer Foundation and the National Children's Home – have begun to extend their work to the 17- to 21-year-old 'young adult' age group. One delegate at

NAPO's AGM accused the Rainer Foundation of introducing some of the Green Paper's proposals 'by the back door' at a scheme it runs in Salford. It would certainly be ironic if the Foundation, which began life as the London Police Court Mission, found itself competing for clients with the agency which took over its original role.

The Green Paper also considers the idea of importing electronic monitoring or 'tagging' from the USA, as a means of enforcing curfews or facilitating the 'tracking' of offenders. Shortly after it was published, the Home Secretary told the Tory Party conference that he intended to apply tagging experimentally to people on bail, since this could be done without waiting for the legislation that would be needed to introduce it as part of a sentence. Neither probation officers nor the police are eager to take on the role of running the computers which monitor the signals emitted by the electronic 'tag', and the Home Office reportedly intends to allot this task to a private company – most likely Marconi – which will report apparent breaches to the police.[74] One of the longest running US schemes, in West Palm Beach, Florida, affords a precedent for the private operation of electronic monitoring. As one American 'consumer's guide' suggests, it may be advisable from the state's point of view to ensure that the firm operating the equipment is independent of any particular manufacturer, so that it will be in its interest to seek out the most reliable technology.[75]

In the USA, the impetus for the development and marketing of this new form of punishment has come mainly from the private sector, and whatever its merits it arguably provides some evidence of the power of the market to stimulate innovations in penal practice.[76] Although experiments were carried out in the 1960s, it is only in the last few years that the prison overcrowding crisis has reached a point where electronics firms have thought it worthwhile to make the equipment commercially available, and there are now numerous variants of the 'tag' on sale in the USA, promoted by glossy brochures and advertisements in corrections magazines. In Britain, too, the private sector has been involved in promoting the idea through the Offender's Tag Association, one of whose principal members is the Technical Director of an unnamed 'leading British electronics company'.[77]

Despite the competitive pressures to come up with ever more sophisticated variants of the 'tag', all the US systems are still beset by considerable technical problems – for example, faulty telephone systems can generate false alarms, as can metal objects like refrigerators which interfere with the signal – and the number of people who can be handled by any one scheme is too small to make a significant impact on local jail populations. But although in the short term the potential for developing electronically monitored curfews or house arrest in Britain may be limited, in the long term there is good reason for the anxieties expressed by some American commentators that the ability of such measures to turn 'every home into a prison and every bedroom into a cell' may portend 'a radical change in the nature of social controls'.[78] One can imagine, for example, what might have happened had electronic monitoring been widely available as a condition of bail during the miners' strike.

Another device for incarcerating people without actually putting them in prison is suggested in the Green Paper on *Private Sector Involvement in the Remand System* which suggests that private companies might operate 'secure bail hostels' with conditions 'such as a 12-hour curfew and a more structured daytime programme' (para. 6). As with the 'supervision and restriction order', the combination of a 'structured programme' by day and a curfew at night could add up to something very similar to 24-hour imprisonment, but there are particular philosophical difficulties in justifying the imposition of a 'structured programme' on people who have not been convicted (even in prison such inmates are exempt from compulsory work). Though ostensibly proposed on grounds of efficiency, the involvement of the private sector could again be a means of circumventing the likely opposition of probation officers. Although the voluntary sector is already involved in providing hostels for offenders or people on bail, these are generally *less* formal and restrictive than the bail and probation hostels run by the probation service,[79] and it is likely that many voluntary organizations would baulk at the kind of regime envisaged by the Green Paper.

CONCLUSION

At the beginning of this chapter we outlined a view of the role of private organizations at the shallow end of the penal system, derived from the historical studies of Donzelot and Garland, and the analyses of contemporary developments in North America by Ericson *et al.* and by Cohen. What this view suggests is that private, voluntary organizations are co-opted into the penal system, submitting to increasing state regulation in exchange for funding and a share in the state's power to punish. In this way, the apparatus of social control is extended into the community, while the involvement of voluntary organizations creates a façade of apparent informality and benevolence. We find this a very plausible account of much, perhaps most, voluntary sector activity in and around the penal system, and indeed of much that is done in the name of 'welfare pluralism' in other areas of social policy. Mike Nellis's work on the voluntary sector in intermediate treatment also broadly supports this view, and so does our own reading of the literature emanating from the Intermediate Treatment Fund, the National Children's Bureau and similar organizations.[80]

As it stands, however, this analysis is too all embracing. It fails to recognize the diversity of political strategies in which voluntary agencies can figure, or to take sufficient account of the conflicts within the penal system. Thus we have seen how, on the one hand, privately managed projects may be set up in a deliberate attempt to blunt the edge of the expansion of social control, to convert a strategy of individualization and normalization to one which seeks to raise awareness of the social and political dimensions of crime and punishment; and how, on the other hand, voluntary or indeed commercial agencies may be used to develop more coercive forms of control in the face of opposition from within the state penal apparatus – either through a process of negotiation and compromise, as in inter-agency IT schemes, or by bypassing state employees in favour of a more pliant, fragmented and vulnerable workforce.

It has to be admitted that examples of 'radical alternatives' are thin on the ground in Britain. There are, it is true, a number of projects connected with the criminal justice system in some way which exemplify the progressive possibilities of the voluntary sector – rape crisis centres, groups for battered women, ex-prisoners' self-help groups and so forth – but none of these is involved in the actual administration of penal measures. There have, however, been some noteworthy experiments in other countries, which although they probably could not be closely replicated in Britain, are worth mentioning to illustrate further the range of possibilities that exists. The type of radical strategy we have outlined has been pursued energetically and imaginatively by Australian ex-prisoners and their allies, perhaps the most remarkable instance being a scheme where offenders on community service worked for the Prisoners' Action Group.[81] In the Netherlands, where the official probation service, like most social services, is a voluntary agency, an alternative, private probation service has recently been established in an effort to preserve some of the progressive practices which were being squeezed out of the official system.[82] And in the USA, despite the difficulties we noted earlier, some quite radical projects manage to survive – for example schemes for offenders which see their role as 'empowering the community'.[83]

While we must always be wary of taking such projects' representations of themselves at face value, we would argue that both the promotion of 'radical alternatives', and the kind of defensive and oppositional work engaged in by some probation officers and social workers, constitute valid responses to the dilemmas which crime and punishment pose for the Left. In saying this, we do not wish to overstate the potential of such strategies, nor are we blind to the power relationships which pervade all activities within the penal complex, however libertarian in intent. All we would claim is that is possible to carve out spaces within the penal apparatus in which 'offenders' are not simply 'normalized', but are encouraged to think critically about their social circumstances and helped in trying to change them. In this kind of work the comparative autonomy of voluntary agencies, and their capacity for an advocacy role and for what Kramer calls 'consumerism' – involving the people on the receiving end of a service in determining how it is delivered – offer distinct advantages.[84]

NOTES

1. Notably N. Tutt and H. Giller, *Manifesto for Management*, Social Information Systems, Manchester, 1987.
2. D. Garland, *Punishment and Welfare*, Gower, Aldershot, 1985, pp. 206, 265–78.
3. J. Donzelot, *The Policing of Families*, Hutchinson, London, 1980, p. 122.
4. Garland, *Punishment and Welfare*, pp. 210–14; D. Bochel, *Probation and After-Care*, Scottish Academic Press, Edinburgh, 1976.
5. W. McWilliams, 'The mission to the English police courts 1876–1936', *Howard Journal*, 22, 1983, pp. 129–47.

6. For an analysis of this form of power in a contemporary context see R. Harris and D. Webb, *Welfare, Power and Juvenile Justice*, Tavistock, London, 1987.

7. S. Cohen, *Visions of Social Control*, Polity Press, Cambridge, 1985, pp. 63–6.

8. R. V. Ericson, M. W. McMahon and D. G. Evans, 'Punishing for profit: reflections on the revival of privatization in corrections', *Canadian Journal of Criminology*, 22, 4, 1987, pp. 355–87.

9. K. Menzies, 'The repid spread of community service orders in Ontario', *Canadian Journal of Criminology*, 28, 1986, pp. 157–69.

10. Our impression is that what we referred to earlier (pp. 29–31) as 'commodification' is much more advanced in Canada than in Britain: in other words, voluntary agencies are assessed much more in terms of their ability to sell services more cheaply than the state can provide them. See, for example, *The Justice System: A Study Team Report to the Task Force on Program Review*, Ministry of Supply and Services, Ottawa, 1985, pp. 301–4.

11. For a trenchant critique of this trend, from a liberal perspective, see R. B. Pinker's dissenting memorandum to the Barclay Report (*Social Workers: Their Role and Tasks*, Bedford Square Press, London, 1982).

12. J. Pitts, *The Politics of Juvenile Crime*, Sage, London, 1988, pp. 64–7.

13. C. Cockburn, *The Local State*, Pluto, London, 1977, pp. 114–16.

14. See H. Blagg and N. Derricourt, 'Why we need to reconstruct a theory of the state for community work' in G. Craig, N. Derricourt and M. Loney (eds), *Community Work and the State*, Routledge, London, 1982.

15. J. Ward, 'Creative conflict,' *Community Development Journal*, 13, 2, 1978, pp. 79–85. See also M. Loney, *Community Against Government*, Heinemann, London, 1983.

16. M. Brenton, *The Voluntary Sector in British Social Services*, Longman, Harlow, 1985, p. 94; N. Johnson, *The Welfare State in Transition: The Theory and Practice of Welfare Pluralism*, Wheatsheaf, Brighton, 1981, pp. 120–21.

17. Probably the most cogent exposition of the welfare pluralist agenda is in R. Hadley and S. Hatch, *Social Welfare and the Failure of the State: Centralized Social Services and Participatory Alternatives*, Allen and Unwin, London, 1981. *Op. cit.*, note 16, both provide useful overviews of the debate.

18. D. Hurd, 'Citizenship in the Tory democracy', *New Statesman*, 29 April 1988; P. Hirst, 'Associational socialism in a pluralist state', *Journal of Law and Society*, 15, 1, 1988, pp. 139–50; J. Keane, *Democracy and Civil Society*, Verso, London, 1988, Essay 1.

19. *Op. cit.*, note 16, Johnson, p. 184.

20. P. Beresford and S. Croft, 'Welfare pluralism: the new face of Fabianism', *Critical Social Policy*, 9, 1984, pp. 19–39.

21. NACRO, *Annual Report 1987/1988; Report of the Council and Accounts, 31 March 1988; Young Offenders and Youth Training*, NACRO, London, 1987.

22. D. Robbins, *Small Gains: Community Projects for Young People in Trouble*, NCVO, London, 1984, p. 18.

23. B. Beaumont, 'Privatization: a time to be alert', *Social Work Today*, 23, March 1987.

24. M. Ryan, *The Acceptable Pressure Group: Inequality in the Penal Lobby, a Case Study of the Howard League and RAP*, Saxon House, Farnborough, 1977. Tony Ward was briefly a member of Newham Alternatives Project's management committee.

25. Radical Alternatives to Prison (RAP), *Alternatives to Holloway*, Christian Action, London, 1972.
26. S. Cohen, Introduction to L. Dronfield, *Outside Chance: the Story of RAP*, RAP, London, 1980.
27. *Ibid.*
28. *Ibid.*
29. M. Ryan and T. Ward, 'Law and order: left realism against the rest', *Abolitionist*, 22, 1986, pp. 29–33.
30. H. Walker and B. Beaumont, *Probation Work*, Basil Blackwell, Oxford, 1981, Chapter 9.
31. P. James, 'Day centres', in H. Walker and B. Beaumont (eds), *Working With Offenders*, Macmillan, London, 1985.
32. *Ibid.*
33. R. Adams, S. Allard, J. Baldwin and J. Thomas (eds), *A Measure of Diversion?*, National Youth Bureau, Leicester, 1981, p. 15.
34. J. Baldwin *et al.*, *Give 'em a Break!*, NYB, Leicester, 1982.
35. J. Adams, 'Pontefract Activity Centre', in *op. cit.*, note 33.
36. *Ibid.*, p. 241.
37. *Ibid.*, p. 263.
38. *Ibid.*, p. 245.
39. *Op. cit.*, note 22, provides an illuminating account of staff/management relations in projects for young offenders. For some advice on how to cloak radical practices in acceptable language see *op. cit.*, note 30, p. 186.
40. A. Leissner, A. T. Powley and D. Evans, *Intermediate Treatment: A Community-Based Action Research Study*, National Children's Bureau, London, 1987.
41. As mentioned in the preface, our discussion of these parallels was stimulated by Mike Nellis's paper on 'The voluntary sector and intermediate treatment', Institute of Criminology, Cambridge, 1987.
42. Intermediate Treatment Fund, *Youngsters in Trouble: The Way Ahead*, ITF, London, 1983, p. 3.
43. T. Locke, *The Involvement of the Voluntary Sector in Intermediate Treatment* and *The Involvement of the Voluntary Sector in Intermediate Treatment in Hounslow*, National Youth Bureau, Leicester, 1981.
44. *Op. cit.*, note 42, p. 3.
45. *Op. cit.*, note 13, pp. 100–1.
46. T. Locke, *The Involvement of the Voluntary Sector in Intermediate Treatment in Southwark*, NYB, Leicester, 1981.
47. T. Locke, *The Involvement of the Voluntary Sector in Intermediate Treatment in Doncaster*, NYB, Leicester, 1981. A more recent account of DITO's work can be found in A. Robinson, *Befriending and Tracking Schemes*, National Childrens' Bureau, London, 1986, which also illustrates the extensive use of volunteers in both the statutory and voluntary sectors.
48. *Ibid.*
49. Cited in D. N. Thomas, *White Bolts, Black Locks: Participation in the Inner City*, Allen and Unwin, London, 1986, pp. 43–4.
50. *Ibid.*, p. 52.
51. NACRO, *Annual Report 1986/7*.
52. J. Pitts, 'Black young people and juvenile crime: some unanswered questions', in R. Matthews and J. Young (eds), *Confronting Crime*, Sage, London, 1986.

53. *Op. cit.*, note 41.
54. V. Blickem and J. Kavanagh, *Community Based IT – Working with Volunteers*, Cambridge IT Partnership, 1982, pp. 7–8.
55. T. Locke, *The Involvement of the Voluntary Sector in Intermediate Treatment in Southwark*, National Youth Bureau, Leicester, 1981, p. 10; *op. cit.*, note 43, p. 2.
56. DHSS, *Circular LAC*, 83, 3.
57. *Young Offenders*, 1980, Cmnd 8045.
58. P. Hope (ed. N. Tutt), *Voluntary Organizations and Intermediate Treatment*, NCVO, London, 1980.
59. NACRO Juvenile Crime Section, *Diverting Juveniles from Custody*, NACRO, London, 1987, p. 3.
60. NACRO Juvenile Offenders Team, *Project Development Survey: DHSS Initiative*, 1985.
61. *Op. cit.*, note 41.
62. Cited in *op. cit.*, note 16, Brenton, p. 8.
63. Denis W. Jones, personal communication.
64. B. Featherstone, *There is an Alternative!*, PRT, London, 1987.
65. *Op. cit.*, note 6, pp. 111–12, 126–7.
66. J. Pratt, 'Juvenile justice, social work and social control: the need for positive thinking', *British Journal of Social Work*, 15, 1985, pp. 1–24.
67. A concept borrowed by *ibid.*, p. 11 from T. Mathiesen, *The Politics of Abolition*, Martin Robertson, Oxford, 1974.
68. J. Pitts, *The Politics of Juvenile Crime*, Sage, London, 1988, p. 113. For a more sympathetic assessment see D. W. Jones, 'Recent developments in work with young offenders', in J. C. Coleman (ed.), *Working With Troubled Adolescents*, Academic Press, London, 1986.
69. *Op. cit.*, note 59.
70. D. Brindle, 'Charities plan care company', *Guardian*, 10 October 1988.
71. J. Pratt, 'Delinquency as a scarce resource', *Howard Journal*, 24, 1985, pp. 93–107.
72. *Op. cit.*, note 23; M. R. Nash and D. E. Delannoy, 'Toothless tagging or supervision that bites?', *Justice of the Peace*, 30 April 1988.
73. A. Ballantyne, 'Hurd considers private sector probation orders', *Guardian*, 23 October 1987; R. Allan, 'Correct me if I'm Wrong . . .', *Social Work Today*, 16 June 1988.
74. *Independent*, 13 October 1988.
75. C. M. Friel and J. B. Vaughn, 'A consumer's guide to the electronic monitoring of offenders', *Federal Probation*, September 1986, p. 12.
76. The US literature on tagging is copious but repetitive. The six papers on the subject in B. R. McCarthy (ed.), *Intermediate Punishments*, Criminal Justice Press, Monsey, NY, 1987, should be more than enough for most readers.
77. Offender's Tag Association, 'The offender's tag', undated mimeo, c. 1987.
78. J. R. Lilly, R. A. Ball and J. Wright, 'Home incarceration in Kenton County Kentucky', in *op. cit.*, note 74, p. 199. See also Blomberg *et al.* in the same volume.
79. *Report of the NACRO Review Group on the Residential Voluntary Sector*, NACRO, London, 1983; J. E. Andrews and B. Sheppard, *Hostels For Offenders*, HMSO, London, 1979.
80. See *op. cit.*, note 41; M. Nellis, 'The voluntary sector and juvenile justice', in *op. cit.*, note 8, Matthews, and most of the texts cited in notes 42–58 above.

81. D. Brown and R. Hogg, 'Abolition reconsidered: issues and problems', *Australian Journal of Law and Society*, 2, 1985, p. 72.
82. The organization VOICES was launched in May 1988. Our thanks to René van Swaaningen for keeping us abreast of developments.
83. L. Curtis, 'Crime prevention: some lessons from the United States', address to the NACRO AGM, London, 1987.
84. R. M. Kramer, *Voluntary Agencies in the Welfare State*, University of California Press, Berkeley, 1981.

CHAPTER 6

Conclusion

There has always been, and indeed still is, a strong tendency among certain academics and practitioners to play down the politics of privatization, to narrow it to an argument about measurable performance or efficiency. The work of Pease and Taylor on the penal system fits into this category.[1] Other commentators attempt to separate political and moral arguments from empirical concerns. For example, when writing about privatization and welfare, Knapp and Judge argue that:

> assumptions about the relative productive efficiency of the public and private sectors . . . are crucial data in almost all decisions about the role and scope for governments, and are subject to a good deal of rhetoric, but little evidence. It is our contention, therefore, that argument about the private and public *production* of welfare should be resolved empirically and, in contrast to justifications for collective financing, largely removed from the realm of political theory and moral philosophy.[2]

While we accept that such a separation does have some analytical value, it should be equally obvious that the two issues are intimately connected. After all, the fact that the 'productive efficiency' of the private sector is being discussed at all is a reflection of changing political and moral perceptions and in any case it is difficult to believe that the 'productive efficiency' of any social institution or service can be sensibly measured by using criteria which are 'largely' divorced from political and moral values.

We make this point about the primacy of political and moral values because it is in these terms that our objections to privatization are mainly framed. That is to say, we have looked at the 'crucial' data about the alleged greater 'productive efficiency' of private penal institutions and found it mostly unconvincing; but the fact that governments might not save money by switching to the private sector is not what concerns us most. Rather, we are more anxious about the ethics of making money out of punishment, about the genuinely difficult

110

political issue of accountability, and about how these anxieties might be accommodated in a future where the state no longer has a near monopoly in the management of punishment and where voluntary non-profit interests play a greater part. It is to the contentious role of the voluntary or non-profit sector in helping to secure that future, and what that future might look like, that we now turn.

In the 1960s and early 1970s, as Cohen points out, the New Left joined with a wide spectrum of liberal opinion in supporting a set of strategies which can be loosely grouped together as the 'decentralization' or 'destructuring' of social control, including the setting up of 'community-based' alternatives to custody.[3] In recent years, the dream has turned sour and an attitude of 'radical pessimism' towards decentralization has become fashionable. Initiatives such as the creation of alternatives to custody or 'community justice centres', in which the non-profit sector has taken a leading role, are now often portrayed as a sinister extension of disciplinary power. As Cohen remarks, most of these radical pessimists, himself included, have relied heavily on the work of Michel Foucault. While we understand the logic of this interpretation, we prefer a reading of Foucault which invites us to see in such developments not *only* an extension of the network of power relations, but also the creation of new opportunities for resistance.[4] Unlike Cohen, we would argue that it is possible, albeit formidably difficult, to set up progressive initiatives 'within the interstices of the criminal justice system',[5] without succumbing to a 'realism' which simply seeks to achieve the existing ends of the system more efficiently and/or humanely.

We realize that by advocating a strategy of working 'in and against' the penal system, we risk the accusation that our position is self-contradictory or even duplicitous, encouraging non-profit organizations to pretend to go along with the aims of the system in order to sabotage it. We freely admit that our attitude towards the state penal apparatus is ambivalent; indeed we believe that such ambivalence is virtually inescapable for the Left. It is hard to deny that many of the diverse kinds of behaviour which are prohibited by the criminal law, such as rape, fraud or burglary, do require some system of rules and sanctions to deal with them; and yet it is equally undeniable that the actual operation of such a system, in a society such as ours, has an in-built tendency to injustice. The best way out of this dilemma which we can see, short of some complete social transformation, is one which attempts to transform the penal system in such a way that instead of imposing some supposed monolithic consensus, it opens up the complex social and moral issues surrounding crime and punishment to debate and negotiation. As Garland puts it:

a progressive penal politics would begin to conceive of a penal object that is neither the 'responsible individual' of the free-market system nor the 'irresponsible client' of the Welfare State. It would also try to envisage means whereby punisher and punished are not always the state and the individual, and whereby the penal relationship is not one of unquestionable ascendancy (either through knowledge or through power). Above all,

111

it would look to penal institutions and practices that will be open about the character of the norms they enforce, their methods of enforcement and their relationship to the social institutions and ideologies they support.[6]

We cannot attempt here to translate this somewhat cryptic guidance into a comprehensive prescription for change, but we would suggest that one modest step in this direction is exemplified by some of the 'radical alternatives' that we looked at in the last chapter. What these examples suggest is that it is possible to create forms of punishment which, while encouraging offenders to face up to the futility and harmfulness of vandalism, burglary, or whatever, also encourage them to discuss and articulate the features of their social situation which may have led them into such activities and the injustice which they may have experienced at the hands of the criminal justice system itself. They also suggest that, for a variety of reasons, these forms of punishment stand a better chance of survival in the non-profit rather than the statutory sector.

Another aspect of a more democratic or pluralistic penal system would be a much greater involvement, at all levels, of people who are not state functionaries or 'experts', but simply citizens. Again, the voluntary sector looks, in principle, a promising vehicle for this kind of change, although this can hardly be said for many of the larger voluntary organizations as they presently exist. Such organizations are often highly bureaucratic and unresponsive to client needs; sometimes they are dominated by the state to such a degree that their voluntary status is little more than a matter of form. Moreover – and this is a crucial objection to the ideology of welfare pluralism – there are serious pitfalls in any attempt to move towards 'participatory democracy' by opening up *opportunities* to participate without addressing the material inequalities that affect people's ability or inclination to take up those opportunities.[7] Despite these reservations, however, the desirability of greater participation is a further reason why we would not wish to argue for a state monopoly over the delivery of punishment.

But this brings us to one of the central problems of this book: how can we reconcile our advocacy of certain forms of voluntary involvement in punishment with some of our stated objections to profit making private prisons? This is a much more difficult question than it might appear at first glance. Consider, for example, the argument that private prisons are unacceptable because of the power which they give to private citizens to influence such matters as parole. The remedy put forward by supporters of privatization is that such decisions might be made by visiting state officials, a practice which already has some parallels within the voluntary sector in the operation of many private halfway houses and voluntary hostels, where staff complain to a visiting probation officer about the behaviour of some of their residents who may then be referred to court and then to prison. Although in the case of the voluntary hostel the final decision is taken by the court and in the case of prison discipline it may be taken by a quasi-judicial body such as a Board of Visitors, the fact remains that in both instances a private citizen has a substantial influence over the outcome and that abuses of that influence can, and do, occur. It could, of course, be argued that there is nothing wrong with a private citizen having this kind of influence so long as he or she does not have a vested pecuniary interest in the outcome. However, the fact that an organization is not run for profit by no means precludes its having a vested interest in decisions of this type; indeed the clearest historical examples of the abuses stemming from such vested interests concern the voluntary bodies which used to run British juvenile institutions. Of course, discretionary powers can be abused for a variety of reasons besides commercial ones, in state as well in private institutions. The crucial question is how those who wield such powers can be held accountable.

We would be on very weak ground if we tried to argue that private institutions would necessarily be less accountable than state institutions are now. What we want is, on the contrary, a far stronger form of accountability within the state penal system. But could not any form of accountability which we cared to impose on state institutions equally well be imposed on private ones? Theoretically, it probably could – but beyond a certain point the result would be that the institution would only theoretically be private. An example of this extreme form of 'publicization' is the concept of the 'controlled community home' under the Children and Young Persons Act 1969. This was a mechanism by which former approved schools could remain in private ownership while being, for all practical purposes, run by elected local authorities who among other powers, would appoint two-thirds of their committees of management. Not surprisingly, the approved school charities found this an unattractive option and if it was not financially possible to preserve a degree of independence, usually preferred to sell their property outright to the local authority.[8] We can easily imagine what a profit making company would have made of such a proposition.

In short, there is a trade off between autonomy and accountability, and the greater the power an agency exercises the greater the priority that must be given to accountability, until a point is reached where private control of the agency becomes either unacceptable or meaningless. Exactly where on the penal continuum this point occurs is not easy to say; but prisons at least are in our view decidedly on the 'wrong' side of it. One of the main reasons for making this judgement is the degree to which prisons rely on direct physical violence: on the capacity physically to overwhelm any resistance on the part of the inmates. We do not rely here on any *a priori* assumption that the state's monopoly of violence can never be delegated, but on the practical impossibility of assessing with confidence whether a private body is fit to be entrusted with such an awesome responsibility. If an inmate is killed – as has already happened in the USA – or seriously injured, it will be a bit late to decide that the contract was awarded to the wrong firm.

An example of the 'grey area' in which lines between acceptable and unacceptable private involvement are less easily drawn is the provision of community homes for young offenders and other children in local authority care. These may well be less oppressive environments than prisons, but they do exercise very considerable power over those in their charge, often for lengthy periods of time. What particularly worries us is that the heads and staff of

113

children's homes play a major role in the review process which determines whether a child will remain in residential care,[9] and either a profit making or a voluntary home could have a vested interest in keeping a child because it needed the fees. Whatever the integrity of the individuals concerned, this is in principle an undesirable position and while we would not go so far as to demand that the state take over all existing private homes, we would not wish to encourage any expansion of the private or voluntary sector in this area. There are in any case reasons for thinking such expansion unlikely.[10]

A further problem about the commercial sector's role in this area is how far it falls within the scope of our ethical objections to making a profit out of punishment. We are sure that the people who run private community homes would be surprised and offended to be told that what they were doing amounted to the deliberate infliction of suffering; but it would be disingenuous to deny that there is an element of punishment in their activities. Where, as it is often the case, the proprietors' profits are no greater than they could reasonably expect as a wage, the point is somewhat academic. But where people are actually getting rich from such operations, defining what they do as welfare rather than punishment hardly lets them off the hook: the public money that is paid to them ought surely to be used for the children's welfare and not to line their own pockets. To those who say that to allow such a distinction is in practice to concede the case for profiting from punishment we can only reply that few issues of principle translate unambiguously into social practice and, in any case, we trust our readers to understand the difference between small-scale private operators who are just getting by and companies like the Corrections Corporation of America – which is more or less where we came in.

But one final word of caution – a warning, we might say, against the dangers of American criminological imperialism. The more this study progressed the more we were struck by the differences between the penal systems we were considering and between the contexts in which they operated: how, for example, the balance between the public and the private sector varied and how within each of these sectors penal arrangements were constrained by different political and legal frameworks, not to mention the cultural legacy of history which has a powerful impact on the way policy makers respond to demands for change. For all these reasons, both the threat posed by the profit making private sector and the potential of the voluntary or non-profit sector as a site for radical intervention, are likely to vary from country to country. To ignore the limitations which this imposes on developing a more general theory would be an error of equal magnitude to some of those which were made in earlier debates about 'decarceration' and 'decentralization': on the one hand, by those who saw all such developments as part of a uniform response to the 'fiscal crisis of the State',[11] and on the other, by those of the New Left who thought that community action in its various forms was of itself sufficient to secure lasting social and political change.

NOTES

1. M. Taylor and K. Pease, 'Private prison and penal purpose', in R. Matthews (ed.), *Privatizing Criminal Justice*, Sage, London, forthcoming.
2. K. Judge and M. Knapp, 'Efficiency in the production of welfare: the public and private sectors compared', in R. Klein and M. O'Higgins (eds), *The Future of Welfare*, Blackwell, Oxford, 1985.
3. S. Cohen, 'Taking decentralization seriously', in J. Lowman, R. I. Menzies and T. S. Palys (eds), *Transcarceration: Essays in the Sociology of Social Control*, Gower, Aldershot, 1987.
4. Parts of Foucault's *Discipline and Punish: The Birth of the Prison*, Penguin, Harmondsworth, 1979, certainly invite a pessimistic reading, but Foucault is at pains to disclaim such defeatist interpretations when elaborating his theory of power and resistance in *The History of Sexuality: an Introduction*, Penguin, Harmondsworth, 1984, pp. 92–8.
5. *Op. cit.*, note 3, p. 374.
6. D. Garland, *Punishment and Welfare*, Gower, Aldershot, 1985, pp. 262–3.
7. A. Gutmann, *Liberal Equality*, Cambridge University Press, Cambridge, 1980.
8. See D. W. Wills, *Spare the Child*, Penguin, Harmondsworth, 1971.
9. Children's Legal Centre, *It's My Life Not Theirs*, London, 1985.
10. M. Knapp, 'Private children's homes', *Policy and Politics*, 15, 4, 1987, pp. 232–3.
11. A. Scull, *Decarceration: Community Treatment and the Deviant, a Radical View*, Prentice Hall, Englewood Cliffs, NJ, 1977.

Index